The Ten Golden Rules of Online Marketing
Workbook

Turn Your Website into a Profit Center

Jay Berkowitz

Copyright © 2009 by Jay Berkowitz

All Rights Reserved

For more information about internet marketing strategies and Ten Golden Rules Internet Consulting, please visit www.TenGoldenRules.com

For a listing of upcoming live internet marketing presentations please visit www.tengoldenrules.com.

For information about permission to reproduce selections from this book, please contact Jay@TenGoldenRules.com

Please visit our website: www.TenGoldenRules.com

Design by: James Ross Advertising

Printed in the United States of America

QUM   10   9   8   7   6   5   4   3   2   1

Acknowledgements

To my wife Bonnie. Thanks for supporting me for so many late nights and so many weekends at the laptop.

To my first client Shari. Thanks for allowing us to share your story.

Table of Contents

Introduction

Chapter 1	There are No Rules
Chapter 2	The Internet is Not Television
Chapter 3	Create a UVP
Chapter 4	If you build it they won't just come
Chapter 5	Subscription Models Survive
Chapter 6	Remember the four P's
Chapter 7	Trust is Golden
Chapter 8	Use the right tactic
Chapter 9	The Best Never Rest
Chapter 10	Lead the Trends
Appendix	Recommended Reading and Additional Resources

Introduction

The Ten Golden Rules of Internet Marketing evolved from a presentation I gave at a Direct Marketing Association meeting in Ft. Lauderdale, Florida, in July, 2003. At the time I was directing the marketing for a $50 Million dot-com called eDiets.com, and I wanted to share my experience with, and enjoyment of, internet marketing with the audience.

I was a classically trained marketer. I had the privilege of working on some of the greatest brands in marketing history including Coca-Cola, McDonald's and Sprint. When the internet came to prominence in 1994/95, I selected a job marketing the website for a shipping company over flashier jobs with a major toy manufacturer and an international restaurant chain. I quickly discovered that the internet was a marketer's dream.

After years of trying to prove the value of television, radio and print advertising, and months of waiting for direct mail program results, the internet brought it all together in real time -- the testing capabilities of direct marketing, the communication power of print and creativity rivaling television and radio.

Internet marketing skyrocketed in the mid 1990's following the invention of the web browser and widening internet access. There were no courses on internet marketing and no books to read. Those of us lucky enough to be involved in the field in the 'early days' had to learn by trial and error. I wanted my presentation to be a short cut for internet marketers, an easy-to-understand how-to course to help people save time in succeeding online.

Following the presentation, I was approached by five or six of the attendees and they said "we need to hire you as a consultant." One of the people who approached me, Shari McConahay, said "We have a small website that I started for my family's costume store in Dania Beach, Florida, called Annie's Costumes. We need some help with email and search marketing." Shari became our first client, and my good friend.

I will tell the story of The Ten Golden Rules of Internet Marketing with a focus on Shari's story -- I think it brings the Ten Golden Rules of Internet Marketing to life to follow a real business and a real website and allows for a real world example for you to use as a model of your own marketing efforts.

Not every business sells something on its website. This workbook contains examples from our own Ten Golden Rules business-to-business communications, and several other case studies from large and small clients.

We'll talk about the art and science of internet marketing, creativity and analysis. We'll look at strategic website design, leading strategies for search engine marketing including natural search engine optimization and Pay-Per-Click advertising, we'll explore measurable media including banner advertising and affiliate marketing, and we'll share dozens of free tools, websites and techniques that work for small retail businesses, like Annie's Costumes, and strategies that form the marketing plans for some of the biggest internet marketing programs in the world.

For the new version of the book we have included updates relevant to the new world of Social Media. We have addressed the strategies for addressing the new socially networked world as well as providing information about Twitter, Facebook, LinkedIn and YouTube.

Since internet marketing is constantly changing, we will keep updates for the book on our website www.TenGoldenRules.com/book. Please visit as often as you wish to read articles, case studies and updates.

And please join the conversation. Comment on our blog, listen to our podcast (links to both at www.TenGoldenRules.com) and please call the podcast with questions and comments, there is a 24 hour digital answering machine at 206-888-6606 and we'll answer your questions on the podcast.

Lastly, an invitation to reach out to me personally to connect, network and do business. Full contact information is available at www.TenGoldenRules.com or connect with me on www.LinkedIn.com/in/JayBerkowitz, www.Twitter.com/JayBerkowitz or www.Facebook.com/Jay.Berkowitz.

Golden Rule #1 – There are No Rules

When I sat down with Shari McConahay at the Annie's Costumes warehouse for our first business meeting, she confessed to me that she was a little confused by internet marketing.

"We tried banner advertising and we got some sales, but we're not sure how well it worked," she said. "We want to try email marketing and I keep hearing that search engine marketing is the only way to go. Another expert told me that affiliate marketing is the only strategy for us. I just don't know what the answer is."

I explained, that in my experience with internet marketing, there is no perfect answer for any one website, and sometimes, one strategy that works well for six months may start to slip in performance after a couple of more months. This is the genesis of *Golden Rule #1 – There are no rules.*

I told Shari that traditional offline advertisers follow a set of rules or conventions. They do research to determine consumer wants and needs. Sometimes they even show consumers ideas for ads in focus groups (small research sessions of 2-12 people) and ask them how they would react to the ads if they saw them on TV. Then they take the consumer feedback, modify the strategies and the creative and produce the ads. Then they air the ads. Some companies do additional research, typically telemarketing phone calls when you are about to sit down for dinner, to determine if they had changed your 'intent to buy' or 'brand awareness' or 'brand preference.'

"I know half my advertising is wasted…"

The father of modern advertising, retail baron John Wanamaker, is credited with this saying "Half the money I spend on advertising is wasted; the trouble is I don't know which half." Marketers believe that, overall, they know what they are doing. Often product sales respond to advertising and marketing tactics, particularly when you have some real news about a product or you clearly communicate a great offer that catches the public's attention and interest. For the most part, marketers share Wanamaker's belief that, advertising and marketing activities seem to have a positive influence on product sales; but, it is hard to measure a direct cause and effect relationship.

In 2002, following my experience marketing big brand websites, I joined an aspiring dot-com company called eDiets. I thought that I could apply my experience successfully marketing brands such as Coca-Cola, McDonald's and Sprint to marketing in this pure internet marketing environment. eDiets didn't sell any physical products at that time. When a customer signed up for an eDiets diet, they received online meal plans, menus, shopping lists and expert advice online. Sophisticated programs used the customer's self-reported height, weight, age, medical conditions and dietary preferences to calculate a unique, recommended diet and exercise plan for each customer.

At the time, the eDiets sign-up process was six pages long. It was designed by a group of male programmers and it used fairly dark colors. The company believed in testing different web designs and different offers and methods of internet marketing. So, I applied my traditional marketing know-how. "Over 90 percent of our customers are women," I theorized, "and our web pages are dark and 'male looking,' plus it takes six pages to sign up for the diet. Let's try a short three page sign up with current, fashionable feminine colors such as the oranges and pinks being used in design and popular magazines."

The head of the IT design department tried not to roll his eyes when he heard my theory. He explained that the current sign-up process had been tested dozens of times and that the current web pages were the product of extensive testing. He was happy to have me develop the new test and prove that they already had a winner.

A:B Testing

I worked with a designer to develop 'my' short three [page sign up with] feminine colors for testing in the real online environ[ment. Once I had the] designs complete and the IT team had incorporated [the changes to] allow a customer to actually sign up for an eDiets di[et, we ran the test] for about one week: half of the people who came to [the site got the six page sign] up (version A) and half of the visitors were presente[d with the] resulting three-page sign up (version B). I asked Sha[ri who was the winner] in the test, that is which version signed up a higher p[ercentage of visitors.] She said "The shorter, three page test with more fem[inine colors."]

I explained, "Much to my surprise, my three-page tes[t did not win. In fact,] the six page, darker colored sign-up process was abo[ut even with the] new test." However, we did discover a very interesting development. One page on the new three-page sign up was very effective in convincing people to sign up for our free eNewsletter. Typically, people who signed up for an eNewsletter would read the articles, our diet success stories and low-calorie recipes and a high percentage of them would sign up for the diet within a few weeks. "So what did you do next?" she asked.

Our next step was to develop a new version of the six step sign-up process with a revised eNewsletter sign-up page. We tested the old six-step process against the new six-step sign up with a revised eNewsletter subscription page and had a new winner! The new process generated more sales and more eNewsletter sign ups, which would result in more sales over the next several weeks.

Shari was excited. She said "OK great, let's start testing sign-up pages." I had to put on the brakes. I explained to Shari that we would be testing the sign-up process in the future, but that would take some time.

I further explained that ***Golden Rule #1 – There are no rules*** represents the strategic approach that you have to take with your internet marketing. You must assume that what works in one industry may not work in your industry, and a design or an offer that works for one website, may not work for your website. Also, something that works today may not be effective in 3-6 months. The powerful thing about internet marketing is that you can test different variables quickly and inexpensively and you can measure the results very accurately.

We were able to test different sales funnels within one week at eDiets because we had more than 100,000 visitors to the website every day. We were among the top five online advertisers in the world and we could run an A:B test.

An Advertising Test

Since Annie's Costumes did not have high traffic year round, they would have had to run the test through Halloween to get scientifically reliable results and it would be too late to apply the test results for their peak season. However, there were a number of variables Annie's Costume could be testing and the results would have an immediate impact on sales and profitability.

For example, Shari had signed a contract to run banner advertising on Yahoo! This advertising contract delivered a fixed number of banner impressions: This meant that Shari had contracted Yahoo to show her banners several thousand times as people surfed around the Yahoo! site. I suggested we should test different banner images to determine which banners received more clicks and more sales. Shari was excited to get testing and she gave me a sample of the banner that they were planning to run for the Yahoo! test.

I explained to Shari that the best strategy for banner advertising was not to test banner advertising, but instead to test banner creative. We developed dozens of different creative designs for the banners. We tested different messaging, different creative and different call to action messages designed to generate a click through to the Annie's Costumes website.

We analyzed all of the different designs for three key criteria:
1. Did they generate a click?
2. Did they generate a sale?
3. Did they generate an entry into the contest and a new eNewsletter subscriber?

Internet marketing is not only about driving traffic to a website. Internet marketing is defined by the ability to measure what works, and to build on your successes.

Ten Tips for Banner Design

1. **Consumers read banners left to right and top to bottom.** You should design your banners with this in mind.

2. **Banners must have a call-to-action, or two.** The best place to put the call-to-action is in the bottom right-hand corner of the banner so you catch the reader's attention and then when he/she has read the banner, he/she comes to the button to click on to take action.

3. **Bigger is Better.** The 468x60 pixel banner is a dinosaur the sooner it clicks itself out of existence the better. Try to buy larger banners such as 728x90, 450x450 pixels, 350x250 pixels and 160x600 pixels.

4. **A picture is worth a thousand words.** Show an aspirational image, top left on the banner to immediately capture the reader's attention. The image should be something the viewer would realistically aspire to, such as a healthy model for a diet ad, not a stick thin runway model, or a nice middle class house, not a mansion.

5. **Banners are like billboards.** Use five to six words maximum in the headline, for smaller size banners, three or four words is better. Write involving headline copy.

6. **Ask a question.** Customers will click on a question that intrigues them, or one they are seeking an answer to. A good question encourages the user to click to find out the answer.

7. **Rich media rocks.** Rich media banners are designs that move, flash, change pictures or words, or those that have an interactive component. You'll get three times the click through and two times the sales, on average, when you use rich media.

8. **Interactivity = productivity.** A button to click, a form to fill out or a link to a free offer will improve performance.

9. **Select colors that stand out on the page.** Is the page white and blue? A black banner will "pop" off the page, get noticed and get clicked at a higher rate.

10. **A home page IS NOT a landing page.** When someone clicks a banner promoting a Harry Potter costume, it is a mistake to send them to the home page of Annie's Costumes forcing them to search again. Develop targeted landing pages with information relevant to the content of the banner, or direct the click to the area of your site with appropriate content.

Action Step 1-1

Visit three of your leading competitors or top performing websites who operate similar business models to your own. Use the Way Back Machine http://www.archive.org to review the development of these sites.
1. How often do they change their sites?
2. Are there any logical design evolutions that would make sense for your website?

Action Step 1-2

Go through the sign up processes for three leading websites in your industry and three leading online companies. If possible go all the way through and purchase their product, if not follow the 'Sales Funnel' right to the final button. At each step, capture a screen shot using the print screen function key on your keyboard. Copy and paste each screen shot into a Paint program PowerPoint or a Word document. Print out these pages in color in the order the consumer sees them on the website and paste them up on a wall or white board. Now do the same with your website.
1. What steps are common throughout the sales funnels you captured?
2. What can you learn from the leaders?
3. Are there any steps that seem redundant in your funnel?
4. Are there any ideas you see in the printouts that you can test?
5. Ask your webmaster to pull a log file or analysis from your web analytics (we will explain analytics in Chapter 8) software and identify where customers are leaving the sales funnel. Are there clues on these pages? Does a disproportionate share of customers leave when you ask for an email address or credit card? Would a long page that users have to scroll down work better as two or three separate steps?

Case Study – The Annie's Costumes Home Page on Wayback Machine

Using the Wayback Machine you see the evolution of Annie's Costumes website through to the introduction of a UVP (has not yet been defined) 'Win a Free Plasma TV in 2003" and the current site.

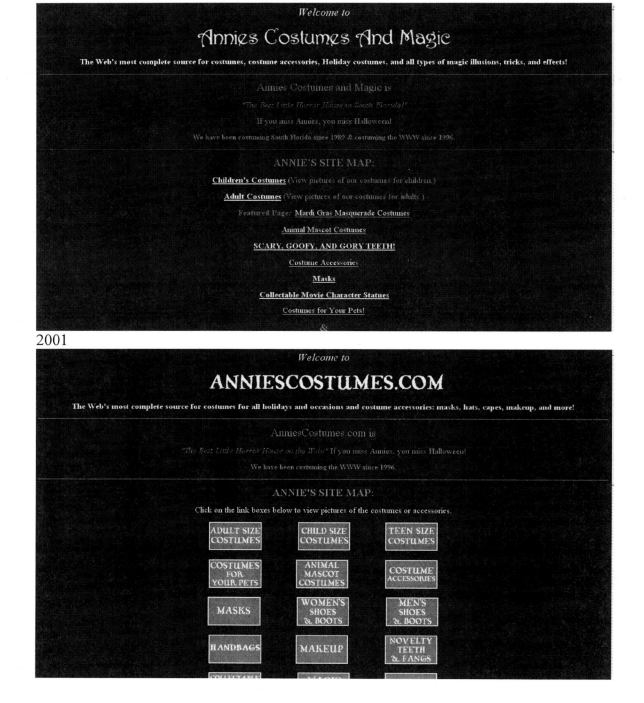

2001

2002

2003

2004

2007

2009

Golden Rule #2 – The Internet is Not Television

Following one of our meetings, Shari and her father and business partner Harold and I went for lunch at a local Mexican restaurant. They knew that I had worked on several advertising campaigns for big television brand advertisers such as Coca-Cola and retailer advertisers such as McDonald's. They were both interested to know if the lessons I had learned in television advertising translated into the job we had to do marketing Annie's Costumes on the internet.

I explained that a common mistake made by most traditional advertising agencies and many website designers was to treat the internet like television – a one way medium that plays video commercials. Television is a very powerful medium to communicate a message, you can tell a story using video, audio, music and demonstration. However, television is becoming a less and less effective tool in the marketer's tool kit. In the 1960's you could reach more than 70 percent of the American television audience by running 31 ads on the three big television networks while countries like Britain and Canada had only one national television network. Today, the game is totally different. There are several hundred television stations, cable networks, TIVO and DVRs and we have tools to zip and zap commercials and other uses for our televisions including playing incredible games and internet access.

I referred Shari and Harold to Golden Rule #2 – The internet is not television. I explained what is meant by this rule: Television was once our most powerful way to connect with customers and prospects, but due to the reduced ability to effectively reach consumers and reduced overall interest in television, the internet was becoming the most powerful way to interact with consumers.

In terms of marketing strategy, the internet is very similar to direct marketing. Direct marketing is defined by the ability to connect directly with consumers vs. intermediaries such as stores and sales people. With direct marketing you can measure return on investment very specifically by campaign or initiative. Furthermore, direct marketing and internet marketing offer businesses the ability to develop and carry on a targeted two-way interaction with consumers who show interest in their products and services. So as the interest and effectiveness of television wanes, smart strategic marketers are applying the strategies of direct marketing - testing different tactics, measuring the effectiveness of different programs, and building their databases - to carry on ongoing dialogues with customers and prospects.

I explained briefly to Harold what Shari and I had discussed weeks earlier when we fist met about the power of testing in the online environment. We had already experienced significant improvement in testing different banner creative and we had begun to put more tests in place. Shari and Harold were beginning to see the value of these strategies, but they still wondered why so many websites, particularly luxury brands and advertising agencies sites, looked like TV commercials.

The Role of the Home Page

I referred to one of the guru's in the internet business, Jacob Nielsen, widely considered the father of website usability. Nielsen, who in his book *Homepage Usability 50 Websites Deconstructed* written with Marie Tahir, explained the role of the home page: "The most critical role of the home page is to communicate what the company is, the value the site offers over the competition and the physical world, and the products or services offered."

When people come to your website, it should be very clear who you are, what you do, and what you expect your website visitor to do to interact with your website.

The worst home page design is a clever 'Flash' style introduction where things whirl and spin with techno music playing. As web visitors, we don't want to watch a weak 60-second video play before we get the information we're looking for. We can't find the 'Skip Intro' button fast enough.

The 8-Second Rule becomes the 4-Second Rule

As the internet evolved, web site developers agreed upon the '8-second rule'. In research tests where internet users were observed interacting with websites, seven to eight seconds was the average time a person would be patient enough to wait for the site to download. As internet access speeds have increased, users have become less patient, and most will only spend four seconds reviewing the information and deciding whether the website they arrive on has what they are looking for and women are even less patient with websites than men.

**You must clearly convey who you are,
what the website offers,
and what specific action you want the user to take.**

As soon as consumers get a bit frustrated trying to find what they are looking for, they start moving their mouse towards the back button and they will return to the search or site that referred them.

Don't fall in love with Flash!

Flash programming can have two very negative impacts on website performance. First, most consumers don't want to watch a simple technology demonstration when they arrive at a site, most try to figure out how to click on the moving image to get into the site. Second, Google and the other search engines can't read Flash well and generally they don't index the content on your site.

In Exhibit 2-1 below, the website for a top advertising agency plays a Flash demonstration when users arrive at the site, there is no clue how to get into the site, the only clue is how to turn the electro music on or off.

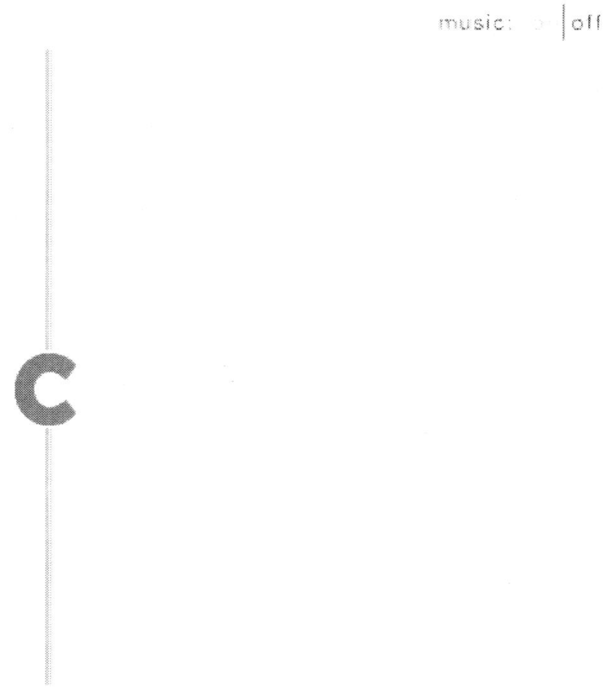

music: on | off

c

Exhibit 2-1

Unlike television, a website is an interactive medium and your goal is to engage and involve site visitors.

The Pareto Principle – Hyper Exaggerated

In 1906, Italian economist Vilfredo Pareto identified the unequal distribution of wealth in his country -- he observed that 20 percent of the people owned 80 percent of the wealth. The Pareto Principle, often called the Pareto Law in business, finds that 80 percent of your revenue will come from 20 percent of your customers. In the online world, the Pareto Principle is 'hyper exaggerated' and in most cases 10 percent of site visitors give you 90 percent of leads (people who come to the site and opt-in for more information but don't buy something) and 1 percent of site visitors deliver 99 percent of sales.

In Exhibit 2-2 below, we ranked a companies top 100,000 customers by revenue and grouped those customers into ranges from 1-1,000, 1,001-10,000 etc. The top three groups represent only 20 percent of the customers and generate 80.3 percent of the company's revenue.

Customer Groups Ranked by Revenue	Revenue Per Group	% of Revenue	% of customers
Top 1000 Customers	$ 1,674,720	40.8%	1.00%
1001-10000	$ 1,028,904	25.1%	9.00%
10,001-20,000	$ 591,067	14.4%	10.00%
20,001-30,000	$ 346,743	80.3%	20%
30,001-40,000	$ 294,372		
40,001-100,000	$ 169,476		
Total Revenue	$ 4,105,282		

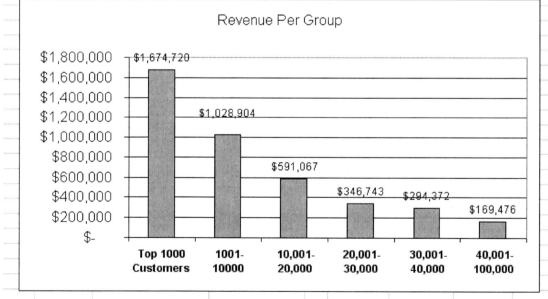

Exhibit 2-2

IDIC – Identify, Differentiate, Interact, Customize

In their 1to1 marketing books, Don Peppers and Martha Rogers write about how companies can customize their entire approach to business with an understanding of individual customers' preferences and behaviors. The concept of 'IDIC' or *Identify, Differentiate, Interact and Customize*, suggests that you should customize a website for your most important individual visitors.

The first step is to identify individuals who represent your best group of customers and differentiate how you treat them. This is the basic principle that the airlines use with Frequent Flyer Clubs. The best customers get special lines to check in, access to comfortable lounges with food and amenities and the first opportunity to receive seating upgrades. What can you do for your best customers? Can they get access to special offers on merchandise before everyone else? Can you give them special access to your experts in exclusive online meetings? Can you build a customized version of your website to meet their special needs? Lastly, you should make special effort to interact with these best customers. Did you collect their birth date when they logged in? Send them a birthday gift. Can you put a special customer service team together to call or email them to address their needs?

You can use internet 'cookies' to identify returning visitors to your website. A cookie is a text string, usually a customer identification number, which your program sends to the user's computer. The cookie is stored in the user's computer browser and the browser returns the cookie to the server the next time the page is referenced. This allows you to identify first time visitors to your site, multiple visitors, registered visitors –those who signed up on the site, returning customers, those who made a purchase, and visitors who responded to special offers. Welcoming first time site visitors, thanking returning visitors for coming back and treating customers differently with a customized greeting are three ideas for customizing your site.

An excellent example of this type of customization is demonstrated by Amazon.com. In Exhibit 2-3 below, Amazon welcomed me back based on the cookie stored in my computer browser. They use my previous buying behavior to make suggested offers to me. There are recommendations for me, pictures and links, and a box called "new for you." There is also an animated "Gold Box" with special deals available only today. This special treatment gives me the incentive to return on a daily basis, and it presents relevant offers to me that improve the likelihood that I will make a purchase.

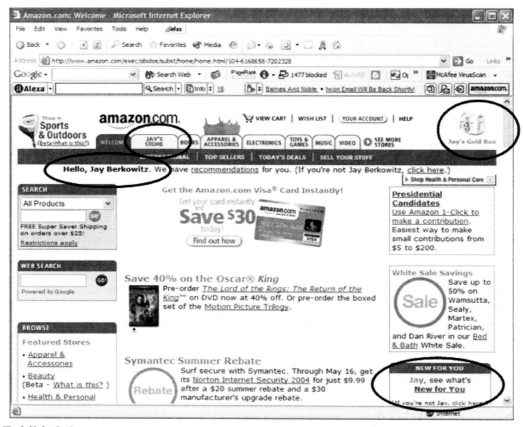

Exhibit 2-3

Cost Per Acquisition (CPA)

In my conversations with the management team at Annie's Costumes, they wondered "Maybe these theories work for large companies, but how did they apply to a small retailer?" I explained that our focus was going to be on six simple letters (CPA/LTV) and two calculations, CPA - Cost Per Acquisition and LTV - Lifetime Value.

Shari asked, "How do we calculate Cost Per Acquisition?" I explained that one of the simplest ways was with Pay-Per-Click search advertising. We can measure, to the penny, how much we spend on a campaign, and we can track conversions, or sales through the online system, then we will simply divide the cost for the ads by the number of sales to determine Cost Per Acquisition. For some marketers who don't sell products online, such as Ten Golden Rules, we measure conversions as people who sign up for an eNewsletter or download a free white paper. Conversions are measured through tracking codes set into the web page that appears after a successful credit card transaction or after an eNewsletter sign up, often called the 'Thank-You' page.

$$\frac{\text{Cost of Advertising}}{\text{Number of Sales or Conversions}} = \text{(CPA) Cost per Sale or Cost per Conversion}$$

You can run a Pay-Per-Click advertising campaign on Google, Yahoo!, Bing/MSN, ASK and dozens of other networks. With Google delivering more than 65 percent of all searches and their system relatively simple to operate, Google is the best place to start a small test. When you log in at http://adwords.Google.com to create an account a credit card is required and you can set up a campaign in about 15 minutes. The system guides you through the selection of the search keywords you want to target (1, 2 and 3 word phrases are often referred to as keywords or keyword phrases), for Annie's Costumes we target keywords like 'Harry Potter costumes' and 'Star Wars costumes' in an example shown In Exhibit 2-4 below, the Annie's Costumes ad appears in the right hand column under 'Sponsored Links.'

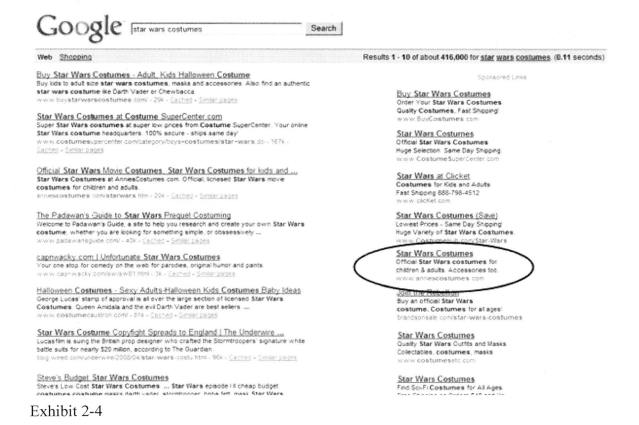

Exhibit 2-4

We use a calculation like the one below (Exhibit 2-5) to measure the cost to acquire a customer through different campaigns. And this same calculation can be used to evaluate different campaigns on different advertising networks and to compare Google, Yahoo! and another network. We ran 100,000 impressions on Google, 50,000 on Yahoo! and 50,000 on a third network. One 'impression' is measured each time our Pay-Per-Click ad is shown, in the Google search above for 'Star Wars costumes' the Annie's Costumes ad shown on the screen is considered one "impression." If the person who did the search clicks on the Annie's ad, that becomes a "click." If the person makes a purchase, we are able to measure a sale.

The Google campaign below in Exhibit 2-5 cost $3,456 and generated 167 sales; the average cost per acquisition was $20.69, slightly better than Yahoo! at $23.30. The other network was a poor performer, so in the second chart we drop the 'Other' campaign and add 50,000 impressions to Yahoo! and reduce our overall CPA to $19.99.

Campaign	Impressions	Clicks	Click %	Sales	Sales %	Cost	Cost Per Acquisition (CPA)
Google	100,000	2234	2.23%	167	7.48%	$ 3,456	$ 20.69
Yahoo	50,000	1189	2.38%	92	7.74%	$ 2,144	$ 23.30
Other	50,000	867	1.73%	57	6.6%	$ 1,756	$ 30.81
Total	200,000	4290	2.15%	316	7.4%	$ 7,356	$ 23.28

Campaign	Impressions	Clicks	Click %	Sales	Sales %	Cost	Cost Per Acquisition (CPA)
Google	100,000	2234	2.23%	167	7.48%	$ 3,256	$ 19.50
Yahoo	100,000	2378	2.38%	184	7.74%	$ 3,759	$ 20.43
Total	200,000	4612	2.31%	351	7.6%	$ 7,015	$ 19.99

Exhibit 2-5

What is a Customer Worth? - Lifetime Value (LTV)

Lifetime Value (LTV) is a calculation we use in internet marketing (and direct marketing) to measure the average value of a customer.

In the example below (Exhibit 2-6) we demonstrate a simple Excel spreadsheet you can use to calculate Lifetime Value. In this example, we acquire 1000 new customers in the first year of the program. Thirty-five percent of these customers make a purchase in the second year. A customer who returns to make a purchase in year two is more likely to purchase again in year three, however despite the increasing return rate, we are only left with 32 of the original 1000 customers after five years. Each customer purchases goods or services valued at $70 and we assume $32 in costs, the net revenue in year one is $38,000 and total five-year net revenue is $60,211. To determine the lifetime value of one average customer, we divide $60,211 by the original 1000 customers to determine the LTV for one average customer of $60.21.

If you don't have accurate statistics or you don't have enough sales history, prepare your spreadsheet based on the best collective knowledge of your team and verify your assumptions against the real market results.

Year	Total Customers	Return Purchase Rate	Gross Revenue	Total Cost	Net Revenue
1	1000	35%	$ 70,000	$ 32,000	$ 38,000
2	350	40%	$ 24,500	$ 11,200	$ 13,300
3	140	45%	$ 9,800	$ 4,480	$ 5,320
4	63	50%	$ 4,410	$ 2,016	$ 2,394
5	32	55%	$ 2,205	$ 1,008	$ 1,197
			$ 110,915	$ 50,704	$ 60,211
				LTV	$ 60.21

Exhibit 2-6

Life Time Value of One Average Customer

LTV = Net Revenue / Original # of Customers

Ten Tips for Pay-Per-Click Search

1. Set up an account at the search engine and start a campaign with a lot of keywords. Use the automated keyword research tools in Google (I recommend starting with Google) and Yahoo! and Bing/MSN to build a list of 300 to 500 keyword phrases.
2. Develop different Ad Groups for specific categories in your business. For example, for Annie's Costumes we would have a Darth Vader Ad Group and a Fairy Costume Ad Group. The ads in each grouping can be very specific to the keyword terms and the ad copy in each group. Different groups allow you to target specific keywords and to create ads that are relevant to the keywords.
3. Set a low daily budget to ensure you don't spend your budget in 1-2 days! A $10 daily budget means that you will spend $300 in your first month. Don't worry when the campaign starts slowly, it normally takes 3-4 days for the campaign to ramp up and start getting traffic in the search engines.
4. Set your initial bid amounts low ($.10 or $.20) to ease into the campaign.
5. The measurement tool will give you feedback on which phrases and ads have a higher click-through rate and more importantly, which phrases generate a higher conversion rate. Delete under performing phrases and add increase bid rates on the phrases that perform well.
6. <u>Definitely</u> set up the conversion tool. The conversion tool gives you a small bit of code your webmaster can add to your Thank-you page, the page that confirms a sale or a sign-up. You will measure sales if you sell something on the site, or measure sign ups for a free newsletter or downloads of a free white paper or free product brochure. (More on free offers in the next Chapter 'Create a UVP')
7. Direct ads to pages which are relevant to the subject matter. For example, ads in the Darth Vader ad group point to the Annie's Costumes page with Darth Vader costumes, instead of pointing to the home page where people would need to search again for Darth Vader costumes.
8. Test a minimum of four different ads. The measurement tools will give you feedback on which ads have a higher click-through rate and more importantly, which ads generate a higher conversion rate. Delete poor performing ads and write new ads similar to the ones that are performing the best.
9. Test dynamic keyword insertion in your ads. In Google, the following code sets the keyword phrase the person searched as the title of the ad, if the keyword searched appears in the ad that phrase appears bold to the viewer and this makes that ad stand out, plus the exact phrase they searched appears as the headline making the ad seem 100 percent relevant to the search. You must also include a default Headline after the "Keyword" because keywords phrases that are longer than 25 characters are too long for the Google headline. An example ad for the Darth Vader Ad Group might be {KeyWord: Darth Vader Costumes}
10. Test phone numbers in your Google ads. Google is the only major search engine that allows this practice, and occasionally people will call the number without clicking, which is a free lead. But here is the most interesting part – a phone number in the ad seems to increase click through and conversion rates, we believe this is because the ads seem more 'real' with a phone number. People know you are a real company not a link site that will waste their time.

"Search is the New Television"

At an internet conference several years ago the keynote speaker declared "Search is the New Television." What she went on to explain was that television used to be the most powerful tool in a marketer's toolkit. Now with more than 100 billion searches conducted each month, her declaration was that online search would become our most effective marketing tool.

More than 90 percent of major purchases are now researched online. If you are selling cars or business services or High Definition televisions or travel or almost anything today, you must be present and prominent in search results. In a study from iProspect and Jupiter Research 39 percent of search engine users believe that the companies whose websites are among the top search results are the leaders in their field.

We search before we buy and we are making a much higher percentage of our purchases online. I purchased my new television with online research, in-store research and an online purchase. I did research online, including Google searches and customer reviews, then I went to a big box store to have a look and speak to the sales people (who seem to know less and less over time) and then I searched for the best price and had my new HD television shipped to me. Another example, according to Rob Chesney, a Vice President at eBay, "a car sells every 53 seconds on eBay"!

Natural Search Engine Optimization

One of the first priorities for Annie's Costumes was to begin to put the pieces in place for success on the "left-hand side" of the search engines. I explained to Shari that the left side or free, organic search engine results are preferred by more than 72 percent of searchers (iProspect Study). While the Pay-Per-Click search is guaranteed traffic, measurable to the penny and great for testing, the long term success of the company would require us to generate a lot of results on the organic side.

Shari was excited, she said "I want the free clicks instead of the paid clicks, let's do search engine optimization!" I promised Shari that one day we would be able to significantly reduce the paid clicks, but unfortunately, natural search engine optimization takes time and effort.

There are more than 100 different elements in Google's mathematical algorithm that determines which websites get listed on page one of the search results and which websites get listed on page 100,000. To simplify the algorithm, there are two really important components.

First you need to have the words people are searching for on your web page. If someone searches for 'Star Wars costumes' you need to have the keyword phrase 'Star Wars costumes' on a page on your website.

Second, you need a lot of activated links *TO* your website. These are underlined links on other websites that link directly to your website. You can measure how many other site link to your website by going to www.AltaVista.com and search "link: www.TenGoldenRules.com" replace TenGoldenRules with the website name you wish to research.

See the Example below in Exhibit 2-7. We'll explain some strategies for building links to your site after we explore how to add words to the site.

Exhibit 2-7

You Can 'Read Your Customers Minds'

Three fantastic tools allow us to "read the minds" of our customers and prospects. Wordtracker, Keyword Discovery and the Google Keyword Tool are products that monitor millions of searches through different automated programs and calculate the number of searches conducted by keyword phrase. In addition, these tools estimate the number of competing web pages that feature each keyword phrase.

The first step for search engine optimization is to select three keyword phrases for each page of your website -- if you have 50 pages on your website you will be targeting 150 keywords. Select phrases that are relatively highly searched with relatively little competition. If your site has only been registered for 1-2 years and doesn't have that many links coming in to it, select phrases with fewer than 1000 competing sites in the analysis. If you have a site with a lot of history and a lot of links you can be more aggressive with the phrases you target.

In the research below (Exhibit 2-8), we find that the keyword phrase 'Halloween costumes' is searched 1280 times (in an average 24 hour period) on Google, 347 times on Yahoo! and 245 times on MSN (now branded Bing).

	Google		Yahoo		MSN		All
Keyword	24Hrs	Competing	24Hrs	Competing	24Hrs	Competing	24Hrs
halloween costumes	1280	5,030,000	347	2,970,000	245	461,087	1872
costumes	1148	58,200,000	311	37,900,000	220	6,502,441	1679
birthday party supplies	596	1,090,000	162	1,630,000	114	121,632	872
renaissance costumes	548	291,000	149	434,000	105	42,491	802
dress up	494	33,500,000	134	9,790,000	94	2,263,634	722
theatre costumes	470	44,000	128	42,000	90	13,285	688
discount party supplies	452	84,000	123	248,000	87	(1)	662
medieval costumes	445	179,000	121	(1)	85	33,185	651
sexy halloween costumes	410	210,000	111	214,000	78	24,130	599
costume wigs	374	403,000	102	525,000	72	63,227	548
dance costumes	370	473,000	100	537,000	71	77,489	541
sexy costumes	370	1,290,000	100	1,180,000	71	157,720	541
kids halloween costumes	353	266,000	96	487,000	68	27,177	517
costume makeup	348	116,000	95	82,900	67	15,232	510
colonial costumes	347	47,300	94	65,100	66	6,371	507
costume	337	95,200,000	92	38,600,000	65	12,413,474	494
dress up games for girls	337	28,400	91	70,000	64	6,053	492
kids costumes	337	662,000	91	973,000	64	60,585	492
costume accessories	334	1,150,000	91	969,000	64	116,310	489
adult costumes	320	1,270,000	87	1,600,000	61	142,057	468
historical costumes	316	248,000	86	197,000	60	28,779	462
pirate costume	309	415,000	84	(1)	59	38,672	452
christmas costumes	304	268,000	82	311,000	58	46,286	444
pirate costumes	297	395,000	81	461,000	57	59,974	435
children costumes	286	404,000	78	533,000	55	11,107	419
theater costumes	283	82,200	77	170,000	54	(1)	414
costume make up	277	(1)	75	80,900	53	13,121	405
easter costumes	275	93,400	75	70,100	53	21,813	403

Exhibit 2-8

If your website is already full of text, you can simply add the target keyword phrases to the copy on the pages. You want to set a target of somewhere between 250 and 1000 words on every page. <u>You need lots of copy on every page on the website, and the home page is the most important page</u>. Include the target keyword phrases two or three times on the page, try to spread these phrases around with one occurrence at the top of the page and one in the middle and one at the bottom. Of course there are several books entirely written about search engine optimization (See our Recommended Reading List at the end of the book). For the beginner, simply adding target keyword phrases and adding a lot of copy will improve your results in the search engines. Below are 10 more tips for search engine optimization.

Ten Tips for Search Engine Optimization

1. Build sites in html or another simple language the search engine spiders can read. If your webmaster or ad agency wants to build a cool Flash website with no attention to search engine optimization, I recommend you find a new webmaster or ad agency. Google and the search engines can't always read Flash. (Note – this is slowly changing, Google announced in June 2008 that they are able to decipher some of the Flash code)
2. "An apple a day keeps the doctor away." Matt Cutts, a Google Engineer and search expert, recommends adding a page of content to your website each day (or every week) to keep the website strong in the eyes of the search engines. You will definitely be rewarded for adding fresh relevant content.
3. Make sure your site has a "site map," a page with links to all of the most important pages on your site. The search engine spiders will look for the words "site map" on any page they land on and follow the links to read and index all of the words on all of the pages on your site.
4. Have a strong on-site link strategy. Try to name main pages of your site with important keyword phrases and use these phrases as navigational links and activated links from other pages on the site to these important pages.
5. Add meta tags to each page on your site. The meta tag "title" is important to search engine results and it should include up to 12 words, the most important one to two keyword phrases and either the company name or website at the end of the title.
6. The meta tag "description" should be 25 to 35 words giving a short, one to two sentence summary of what's on the page. Include a call to action as this often shows in search results. The meta "keyword" tag can include 12 keyword phrases, including the company name/website. Do not repeat any single word more than four times.
7. Header tags are also very valuable for search engine optimization The H1 tag forms a headline on the page and tells Google the words in the tag are important. It should be three to six words, and form the title of the page. Include main keyword phrase in this tag. H2 tags are the subheadings on a page and additional section headers. The H2 tags can be 6 to 12 words long and they should include secondary phrases in these tags.
8. Every image and hyperlink on a page (and there are typically many) offer an opportunity to introduce keywords to the page. Add image names and alt-text. Naming images on your website and including the "alt tags" helps search engines because the engines can't "read" pictures, but they can read the names of pictures, links and the alt-tags.
9. Target a keyword density of approximately 5 percent. Keyword density is the ratio of the number of occurrences of a particular keyword or phrase to the total number of words in a page.
10. You can break up a keyword phrase. Using <u>best health insurance coverage</u> as the example, separate keywords with a period. For example: It's not always easy to find the <u>best health insurance. Coverage</u> can vary depending on the provider.

Link Building

Links to your website are absolutely critical to natural search engine performance - the number of links to your site and perhaps even more significant, the relevance and importance of those links. Relevance is determined by the types of sites linking to your site as determined by the keywords on those sites. For example, sites about costumes and Halloween are valuable sites to have links from for Annie's Costumes. Important sites are extremely valuable to have linking to your site, media coverage and links from USA Today or the Wall Street Journal rate highly in search engine algorithms, industry associations such as The National Costumers Association are valuable for Annie's Costumes as are universities and government websites as designated by .edu or .gov extensions.

There are a number of ways you can get other sites to link to your website, and gain importance in the eyes of the search engines. The best links occur naturally, when you have great articles and amazing content on your website and when other sites link to your site and say there is a great article on link building over at www.TenGoldenRules.com

Ten Tips for Link Building

1. Develop amazing free tools on your website. Free articles, free white papers and free research are great content that other sites will reference and link to your website.
2. All vendors and suppliers are great targets to request a link from their site to yours.
3. Press Releases are a great for building links to your site, when another website or blog refers to your press release they generally link to your site.
4. Article submission sites will make your articles available free of charge to other websites who must include your reference information and a link to your site. The biggest article submission site is eZineArticles.com and there are many others available by searching "article submission."
5. Ask for links from industry associations, we never list our company as Ten Golden Rules; we always list our company name as http://www.TenGoldenRules.com.
6. Your local Chamber of Commerce or Board of Trade is a great place to get a link.
7. When you are requesting a link from a sophisticated web operator, ask them for an anchor text link. A blue underlined activated link Internet Marketing Agency is more valuable than a link www.TenGoldenRules.com
8. List your site in DMOZ.org. This is the original free directory that Google and other sites used in the early days. Once you submit your site, be patient, the directory is administered by volunteers and it may take several months to get listed, re-submitting may put you to the back of the list. And, list your website in directories such as Yahoo!, Best of the Web and Business.com. There is a small submission charge, but for highly ranked sites like these it is worth it. Search for free directory submission sites such as www.JoeAnt.com and www.Skaffe.com.

9. Find out your Google Page Rank. Google gives each site a number between 0 and 10. New sites get a 0 and a very few sites with millions of important links to them are rated a 10. Google interprets a link from page A to page B as a vote, by page A, for page B. But, Google looks at more than the sheer volume of votes, or links a page receives. It also analyzes the page that casts the vote. Votes cast by pages that are themselves "important" weigh more heavily and help to make other pages "important." Google offers several functions on a free toolbar including a page rank calculator at www.toolbar.google.com, then you can analyze your site, competitors and watch your page rank improve every three months as you get more links to your site.
10. Create pages in Web 2.0 sites such as Wikipedia, Facebook, Squidoo, news site Digg.com and tagging site Del.icio.us. Not all of these sites carry search engine link value (some sites designate their links as "no-follow links" telling the search engine not to credit these links in search engine algorithms) , but if when you get listed on high traffic pages a link to your site will drive free traffic.

Action Step 2-1 – Search Engine Optimization

1. Use Wordtracker to build a target keyword list for your site
2. Select three keyword to target on each main page on your site
3. Add each target keyword phrase to the copy three times on each page
4. Submit your site to DMOZ and then submit to ten directories to request links each week.
5. Develop a plan to add a page of search engine optimized content to your site every day, or every week.

Action Step 2-2 – Link Bait - Advanced Link Building Tactic

Link Bait is an industry term for something you add to your website to 'bait' other websites to link to you, in a good way.

One link bait tactic is to develop a list of the top 25 websites or blogs in your industry. Find the sites or blogs through Google or blog searches on specialty search engine Technorati and Google searches in the blog link. Select the 25 blogs with the highest rating in Technorati, the highest profile in your industry and the highest Google Page Rank. Create an article or page on your website and list the Top 25 Blogs. Email each blogger to let them know that they have been selected to the list. A high percentage of those bloggers will link to your site to tell everyone that they have been selected to this exclusive list.

Case Study – Annie's Costumes

After almost five years of search engine optimization, Annie's Costumes has more than 3,000 links to their site! According to SEO Digger (Exhibit 2-9), a free analysis tool, the site has more than 5,400 search engine results that come up in the first two pages of Google. Most important, the site received over 1.2 million FREE visits to their website in one month from Google alone!

Exhibit 2-9

Additional Learning

The following resources are great for learning more about Search Engine marketing:

Our Podcast interview with Google's Matt Cutts:
http://podcast.tengoldenrules.com/10goldenrules-podcast-episode16.html

"Search Engine Visibility," Shari Thurow wrote a classic book on the basics of designing a website for free search engine pick up.

http://www.searchengineland.com. Danny Sullivan and the team at Search Engine Land cover the breaking news in the search marketing industry

Matt Cutt's Blog, http://www.mattcutts.com/blog. Google Engineer Matt Cutts is one of the most respected experts in the search engine space.

Golden Rule #3   Create a UVP

Over the past couple of years they have been working on a redesign project for several of the Annie's Costumes websites. (Note - If you are reading this in 2010 and the site still hasn't been updated, it wasn't Shari's fault, it was the web developer, I promise.)

We discussed several of the main principles we wanted to apply to the site design. As consumers, we have high standards for the websites we visit. We demand a clear layout and an easy to use navigation. We expect to find what we're looking for within three or four clicks. And we are critical judges, voting with our mouse, frustrate me and I'm gone -- I'll hit the back button and return to the search engine I found the site on and click another selection.

I bought Shari a copy of Steve Krug's tremendous book on website design and usability called "Don't Make Me Think." (Author's note, you may also wish to listen to an interview with Steve Krug on Ten Golden Rule of Internet Marketing Podcast #10 found at http://podcast.tengoldenrules.com)

> *"'Don't Make Me Think'. I've been telling people for years that this is my first law of usability…It means that as far as humanely possible, when I look at a web page it should be self evident. Obvious. Self-explanatory. I should be able to 'get it' – what it is and how to use it – without expending any effort thinking about it."*

As website planners and designers, it is imperative that we direct the user. We must make it clear what action we want them to take on the site. One area of the home page should clearly stand out to the site visitor and encourage him/her to click and take this desired action.

Several areas on a website have become conventions or standards – we look for certain things in certain places. Perhaps the most common convention is the position of a logo in the top left corner of a website. Web users now understand that if they are anywhere on a website, they can return to the home page by clicking the logo in the top left position. We expect the website navigation to be on the left of a website or across the top.

A second convention is the location of the search box. 20 percent to 30 percent of web users are searchers -- they like to find the search box when they come to a site and search before they click links or read copy, they look for the search box in the top right corner of a website.

Possibly because of the early days of the world wide web where everything was free and/or because of the open standards of the web, site visitors expect to get a lot of information and tools for free. Consumers hold websites to a higher standard than any other medium. We don't expect our newspaper or magazines to be delivered for free. We don't get a free one month product trial when we go to a retail store. However, when we visit a website we expect something of value for nothing.

Golden Rule #3 - Create a UVP (A Unique Value Proposition). A UVP is the strategy to give your site visitors an incentive to engage with you when they visit your site. Examples of a UVP include a free sample, a free tool or valuable product or service demonstration. The objective is to create something of a high perceived value that the consumer will download or sign up for, or you create a tool or service that web visitors will return for again and again, even bookmarking your site.

An important component of most UVP offers is to encourage consumers to opt-in to receive future special offers and marketing communications from you. Typically this can be achieved by offering a chance to subscribe to a free eNewsletter, or the offer of exclusive promotions and specials.

The Annie's Costume's UVP's

One of the main priorities we had for Annie's Costumes was to start building a database of customers and prospects. We developed the first UVP in a brainstorming session in late summer 2003. Flat screen televisions had just started dropping in price and so we agreed to give away a flat screen TV to one entrant selected in a drawing among all entries in a contest, this would be the first UVP we would test.

At the same time, we devised another small UVP. All contest entrants would be required to complete a short poll telling us their favorite costume by categories such as infants, boys, girls, men's and women's costumes. Everyone who entered the contest and completed the poll was given an opportunity to 'opt-in' to receive future information from Annie's Costumes about other promotions and specials and a high percentage of entrants opted-in.

This approach was a big hit! A high percentage of visitors to the site took our poll and entered for a chance to win a prize that was one of the most desired items by consumers at that time. We quickly built a database of people who were interested in costumes. As I explained to Shari, online retailers are really in the direct marketing business and her database of opt-in customers was going to become one of her most valuable assets.

We had two objectives for the poll results. The first objective was to create a list of the most popular costumes, by category. In 2003 lots of moms came to the site to buy a Harry Potter costume for their sons but they had no idea what to buy their infant daughter. Our lists of the top costumes (See Exhibit 3-1 below) created a simple way for site visitors to shop for the most popular costumes. As soon as we added the list to the website, we started to see an increase in orders and an increase in the number of orders with multiple items purchased.

Exhibit 3-1

The second objective for the poll results was to create a series of press releases about the most popular costumes. We targeted mainstream media with press releases about the most popular costumes for children and we sent lists of the top adult-themed costumes to edgy morning shows such as Howard Stern. This tactic was also a big success. The list and the costumes were featured on television shows including Good Morning America. Shari was interviewed by dozens of media including live radio shows. The story appeared in national print media including an amazing full-page story in USA Today. The day the story ran in USA Today (See Exhibit 3-2 below) was perfect for Halloween sales, October 14, just 16 shopping days left before the big day, and that day became a record sales day for the company.

Exhibit 3-2

As Halloween came closer, we emailed all of the contest entrants two times. The first email announced the initial list of the Ten Most Popular Costumes, by category. The second email, just two weeks before Halloween, offered customers $5 off any costume. Both emails generated significant sales volume for Annie's Costumes, our UVP had worked like a charm!

Over the years we have developed several UVP's for Annie's Costumes. We have tested contests and offers and free downloads. The most important way to think about a UVP for your customers is to offer something of real value, and to start to build a two-way trust based relationship. Send them something they want, special exclusive offers and articles with smart, well written valuable content. Your goal is not only to avoid an un-subscription, but to build awareness and respect for your brand.

UVP's work in all business categories and for all types and sizes of businesses

One example of a successful UVP is the Free Trial. For years, AOL built the largest base of internet service subscribers by mailing out free CDs offering consumers a free trial. We all received countless mailings and samples of the AOL CD offering "45 Days Free." By the time you downloaded the software, figured out how to use it, sent emails to friends or business associates and distributed your me1234567@aol.com email address your free 45 days were up. There was only a low chance you'd stop the service at this point, and besides you now had a copy of AOL Version 17.3 with the free AOL widget you couldn't possibly do without.

Another type of UVP's is created through the compilation and analysis of the actions of website users. Amazon.com has created a fantastic tool called "customers who bought this book also bought." This tool allows users to click on a link below a book listing and see several other books purchased by those who purchased the original book. It produces great results. For example, in the sample below, I researched one my favorite business books "Enterprise One to One" by Don Peppers and Martha Rogers, the UVP tool suggested a book by Seth Godin and I ended up making a purchase because of this tool. This is not only a great business tool. Every year for my wife's birthday I add a couple books to her gift. This past year I entered a favorite, but obscure, book on Josephine Bonaparte, wife to Napoleon. The "customers who bought this book also bought…" section gave me five suggestions, three of which I purchased. My wife loved two of them.

Enterprise One to One: Tools for Competing in the Interactive Age
by Don Peppers, Martha, Phd. Rogers

List Price: ~~$17.50~~
Price: **$12.25** & eligible for **FREE Super Saver Shipping** on orders over $25. See details.
You Save: $5.25 (30%)
Availability: Usually ships within 24 hours

85 used & new from $0.99

Look inside this book   **Edition:** Paperback

Other Editions:	List Price:	Our Price:	Other Offers:
Hardcover	$24.95	$24.95	**160 used & new** from $0.01

READY TO BUY?
Add to Shopping Cart
or
Sign in to turn on 1-Click ordering.

MORE BUYING CHOICES
85 used & new from $0.99

Have one to sell? Sell yours here

Add to Wish List
Add to Wedding Registry
Don't have one?
We'll set one up for you.

Customers who bought this book also bought:

- *The One to One Fieldbook: The Complete Toolkit for Implementing a 1To1 Marketing Program* by Don Peppers, et al (Paperback)
- *One to One B2B: Customer Development Strategies for the Business-To-Business World* by Don Peppers, Martha Rogers (Hardcover)
- *The One to One Manager: Real-World Lessons in Customer Relationship Management* by Don Peppers, Martha, Phd Rogers (Paperback)
- *Permission Marketing : Turning Strangers Into Friends And Friends Into Customers* by Seth Godin (Author), Unknown Unknown (Illustrator) (Hardcover)
- *The Loyalty Effect: The Hidden Force Behind Growth, Profits, and Lasting Value* by Frederick F. Reichheld, Thomas Teal (Paperback)

▶ **Explore Similar Items:** 19 in Books, and 1 in Music

Exhibit 3.3

Another great example of a UVP is The New York Times Archive. The prestigious newspaper invested considerable time and money to digitize every article ever published in its history. A search on the website will turn up articles matching your subject area and the first paragraph is available for free. If you want to purchase the entire article, however, it costs $2.95 and pictures are available for sale as well.

Exhibit 3-4

At eDiets.com we developed a UVP that would be copied on many websites: the "Free Diet Profile". The Free Profile provides consumers with a free analysis based on their answers to a set of questions. In most uses of this tool, the website will offer the site visitor a number of products and services to "opt-in" for while they complete their profile questions. Most sites offer a free email newsletter and many promote offers for other companies such as free trials, newsletters and special price offers. These offers for other sites have become known as "co-registration" in the internet industry, the consumer registers for another companies offer on the original company's website. Some examples of these co-registration offers can be viewed on the free profile on eDiets.com, Beliefnet.com and when signing up for a free Hotmail account on MSN.com.

UVP's work effectively in Business-to-Business environments as well. Many business websites offer a free download of a white paper or product brochure and they will encourage prospects and customers to sign up for their newsletter or special offer emails when they register for the free white paper.

At TenGoldenRules.com, we consistently test different UVP's on our website and landing pages. We offer a free subscription to our Ten Golden Rules Internet Marketing Newsletter, we provide a chapter of this book for free and we offer a free download of the Ten Golden Rules of Online Marketing PowerPoint slides. We have tested many other free offers including a free website overview, a free broadcast of one of my internet marketing presentations and free podcasts. Find out what UVP's we are currently testing at www.TenGoldenRules.com

Ten Tips for Testing

1. Test Offers – Testing different offers will yield the most improvement in most internet marketing programs. Test different prices, test added value offers and test different approaches to increase the perceived value of your products or services.
2. A:B Testing – This is the strategy of testing one offer or design on one page on a website, and testing a second offer or design on another page on the website. Direct an equal amount of visitors to each of the two web pages and measure the effectiveness of each page against your key success criteria (sales, leads, downloads).
3. Test Media – Test different media advertising on other websites with banners and links, email promotions, affiliate marketing, Pay-Per-Click advertising. Measure each media on the return on investment and cost to acquire a lead or deliver a sale.
4. Test Banner Creative – Test different creative designs and different offer messaging. Develop interactive and rich media creative.
5. Test Landing Pages – Test different designs, different offers and different action buttons. Test long landing pages with extensive copy, testimonials and product benefits vs. a short quick call to action landing page.
6. Test Sales Funnels – Develop new designs for each page in the 'sales funnel,' the pages a visitor goes through to sign up for your offer or purchase your products.
7. Test Pay-Per-Click – Test ad copy, test hundreds of different keywords, test bid amounts and ad positions, try different URL's in the ad and test different landing pages.
8. Test Unique Value Propositions UVP's – Test different offers designed to encourage customers to sign up to receive something of a high perceived value in exchange for their email address and contact information. Ask them to opt-in to receive a free eNewsletter or special offers and promotions by email in the future.
9. Test Web creative – Test different website designs, different calls-to-action and different messaging on the site
10. Dip your toe into social media and video. Once you have developed a strong media program, you have tested offers and your Pay-Per-Click program is running well, launch a blog and test some of the new media. YouTube videos are a great way to demonstrate your products, build a Facebook Page for your company.

Action Step 3-1: Create A UVP

The second step to great internet marketing, after driving traffic to your website, is developing your UVP. What can you offer your customers that would truly be valuable and remarkable? Do you have some research you did that you can package up into a Free White Paper? Can you develop a rate calculator that consumers could use to compare products in your industry? Can you hire an expert to write a guide that you can offer for a free download? What is the most unique and compelling contest that you could promote on your website?

Once you get someone to act on your UVP offer treat them with an incredible amount of respect. Don't spam them with email offers that are available to anyone. Send them valuable information, unique promotions and special offers in the form of an eNewsletter. Once in a while, surprise them. Send an email with a special chance to do something unique or a chance to claim a free prize just for reading to the end of your email.

Case Study: Tax Action Plan

We developed a UVP for a specialty tax accountant. The UVP offered a FREE Tax Action Plan (Exhibit 3-5), a customized analysis prepared for everyone who completes a form on the right-hand side of the website.

The forms generated a very high lead percentage and the highly valuable tax actions plans built trust and understanding of the specialized level of expertise this firm provided. A significant percentage of people who received Tax Action Plans from the firm have become regular clients.

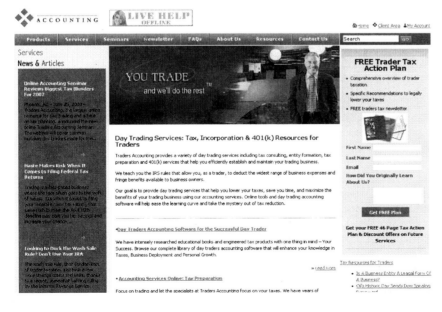

Exhibit 3-5

Golden Rule #4 - If you Build it They Won't Just Come

In the Spring of 2004, Shari and I were both on a panel for a Chamber of Commerce business function. After the event we went for lunch with a few of the attendees. Many of them were frustrated because they felt they had a lot to offer people on their websites but they didn't get enough people visiting the site.

Shari was really catching on to the Ten Golden Rules at this point and she said "If you Build it They Won't Just Come. You need to push, pull and drag people to your website." I was beaming with excitement!

I explained to the group that the dot-bombs of the late 1990s and early 2000, the big web companies that ceased operation in the web crash, made the mistake of assuming that they could build a great website and the riches would soon follow.

Many of these companies built incredible websites. They featured fantastic functionality, they had robust systems and they provided tremendous tools. However, many of them spent their IPO millions building the websites and they didn't have the money left or the know-how to bring consumers to the sites.

Several of these companies tried to use traditional offline advertising to drive traffic to their websites. Many went so far as to run multi-million dollar Super Bowl ads to build their brands. Offline advertising is very expensive because many advertisers use this method to build their brands, they don't measure their return-on-investment like direct marketers.

When you are promoting a website with offline advertising you have three challenges:
1. You need to create demand for your product or service
2. You must generate intent for prospects to come to your site
3. They must remember to come to your site the next time they are at a computer.

With advertising on the internet you only need to create enough intent or impulse to get them to click a link to come to your website. As the internet has evolved, there are two significant ways to get traffic without paid advertising: The first is Search Engine Optimization (covered in Chapter 2), and the second is viral events. Viral marketing is named after a virus that spreads form person-to-person.

There are also many types of paid advertising on the internet, including banner advertising, links, Pay-Per-Click search advertising, email (legitimate opt-in email and illegal spam), partner marketing, social media marketing and affiliate programs.

Push, Pull and Drive Consumers to your Website

Very few sites can succeed on word-of-mouth referral and natural search engine results alone: You must push, pull and drive consumers to a website.

Search Engine Marketing

We explored the two main types of search results, Pay-Per-Click and natural results in Chapter 2. The natural or 'organic' search results are the results on the left side below the Sponsored Links Pay-Per-Click results are the ads at the top and the right hand side of a search page that are clearly identified as 'Sponsored Links."

The Role of Pay-Per-Click (Paid Search)

While most web users prefer to click on the left side, many do click on the paid ads. Sometimes they can't find the results they want on the left or they're looking for a business and they want to click on a paid ad. Others click on copy that catches their eye.

Some advertisers are scared of paid search they worry that everyone will click on their ad and it will cost a small fortune. In most cases the opposite is true. You can select hundreds of keyword phrases, the more specific the phrase often the better it will perform, you can set low per-click bid rates and daily budgets to guard against a wave of traffic and then your ads will be shown to people actively searching for your products and services.

Pay-Per-Click advertising can be a very cost-effective method of driving traffic to your site. You select the keyword phrases you want to advertise on, you select the exact words that you want to use in your ad (they will restrict some things like BOLD copy and superlatives such as The Best) and you set the bid rates to determine where your will be shown. Paid search is an auction environment, where you are able to bid more 'per click' to determine how high on the page your ad appears. You are able to track how many times your ad was shown, how many clicks you received, and how many people took a specific action on the site such as making a purchase or signing up for a newsletter.

The example below (Exhibit 4-1) is from one part of the Ten Golden Rules Google paid search advertising campaign. We have written the ad copy which appears on the top left (there are actually six different ads in test). We have selected a group of keywords for this test which appears on the left. We can set a bid rate for each keyword phrase and the program shows me that my ads have been shown to searchers 2,104 times (this is the ad impressions or Impr. in the middle column.) 28 of these searchers who saw the ad clicked on it at a 1.3 percent Click Through Rate (CTR). The average Cost Per Click (CPC) is $0.80. Even though we are bidding more than $1 for most of the keyword terms, we are only charged 1 cent more than the bid below our bid. The cost for this portion of the campaign during this time period was $22.26 and the ads appeared, on average, in position 9.3 (this is on page 1 near the bottom).

The most important statistics are the conversion rate (Conv. Rate) and cost per conversion (Cost/Conv). Google allows you to track specific actions that visitors take on the site. After they click on our ads, 25 percent of them signed up for our newsletter at an average cost of $3.18 each. If we wanted to, we could measure the number of sales or the number of downloads of a white paper or any other specific action on the site.

Keyword	Status [?]	Current Bid Max CPC	Clicks	Impr.	CTR	Avg. CPC	Cost	Avg. Pos	Conv. Rate	Cost/Conv.
Search Total	Enabled	Default $1.00 [edit]	28	2,104	1.3%	$0.80	$22.26	9.3	25.00%	$3.18
internet advertising	Active	$1.00	5	907	0.5%	$0.75	$3.75	14.1	20.00%	$3.75
"search engine submission"	Active	$1.27	2	372	0.5%	$0.94	$1.87	6.0	50.00%	$1.87
"marketing on internet"	Active	$1.50	3	8	37.5%	$0.56	$1.66	4.2	33.33%	$1.66
"internet marketing conference"	Active	$1.00	2	12	16.6%	$0.79	$1.58	4.7	50.00%	$1.58
"internet marketers"	Active	$0.96	2	15	13.3%	$0.75	$1.50	4.3	50.00%	$1.50
"internet marketing firms"	Active	$1.00	1	5	20.0%	$0.76	$0.76	5.4	100.00%	$0.76
internet presentation	Active	$0.96	1	88	1.1%	$0.96	$0.96	6.7	0.00%	$0.00
"internet marketing center"	Active	$0.56	1	48	2.0%	$0.79	$0.79	3.6	0.00%	$0.00
"internet marketing companies"	Active	$1.50	0	36	0.0%	-	-	9.6	0.00%	$0.00
"marketing on the internet"	Active	$1.27	0	36	0.0%	-	-	5.5	0.00%	$0.00
"marketing and internet"	Active	$1.00	0	27	0.0%	-	-	3.8	0.00%	$0.00
"internet marketing tips"	Active	$1.50	0	22	0.0%	-	-	3.8	0.00%	$0.00

Exhibit 4-1

There are two places you can run Pay-Per-Click advertising. The more commonly known type of paid search ads are shown when you do a search on a search engine such as Google, Yahoo! or Bing/MSN. The second category of paid search is called contextual advertising. These ads are shown on high traffic websites and the ads displayed are based on what the web site is displaying. For example, if the site is a movie review site the ads might offer DVD Movies for sale. If the person clicks on the ad, the web site shares the click revenue with the search engine. The results of the contextual portion of the campaign can be very different from the search engine part of your campaign. We recommend turning off contextual advertising in new campaigns until you establish your campaign CPA and then testing the contextual ads. An example of contextual AdSense ads below in Exhibit 4-2.

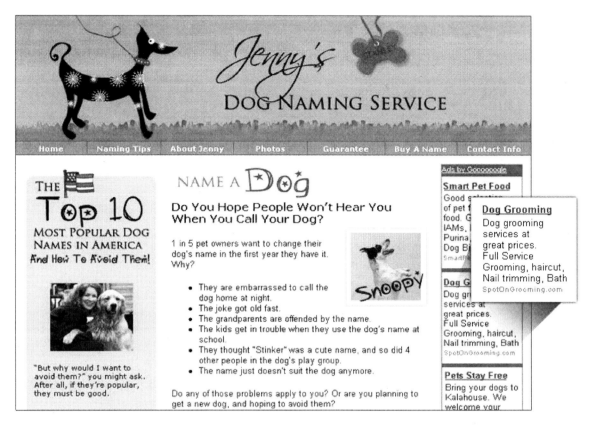

Exhibit 4-2

Traditional Advertising

Traditional advertising including television, radio, magazine, newspaper and direct mail have been used to drive traffic to websites with mixed success. When the internet was growing, there wasn't a lot of traffic online and using traditional media to build internet brand awareness was the preferred tactic. Many dot-coms used traditional advertising including some infamous Super Bowl commercials such as the Pets.com sock puppet, to fuel brand awareness. This strategy has been used with moderate success by brands such as Overstock.com, Buy.com and GoDaddy. Domain name registrar GoDaddy was largely unheard of until they used sexy spokes models on the Super Bowl games to build awareness of their low-cost website name registration service.

For most companies, Super Bowl ads costing over $3 Million for creative and media are not in budget. In many cases, a multi-million dollar budget is required to build website name awareness and intent to purchase online.

Integrate all Offline Activities to Point Traffic to your Website

Most companies have recognized the value and importance of driving traffic to their websites. The best traffic is free traffic, which comes when a visitor types in your website address, clicks on a link on another site or the clicks on the free search results linking to your site.

Over the past several years companies have been shifting the focus of their advertising from promoting a 1-800 number to presenting their website on television, radio and in print advertising. All paid advertising should include your web address and you should give people a reason to visit. For store hours and locations visit www.website.com. To see our weekly specials please visit www.website.com.

Companies should do everything they can to integrate all offline activities and point traffic to their websites. Every brochure, label, letterhead, envelope, sticker and sales collateral should include a prominent listing of the company website with a reason to visit. See our Special of the week at www.website.com. Get a Free White paper at www.website.com. Download free software at www.website.com.

Another simple and effective strategy is to ask every employee to include a link to your website on their email signature. Emails can be forwarded to hundreds of individuals and an effective signature can generate free traffic. This is also an effective strategy when participating on internet forums and discussion groups. Signing your name with a website address can also generate free clicks.

Affiliate Marketing

Affiliate Marketing is a model in which a business rewards an affiliate for each visitor or customer brought to the business by the affiliate's marketing efforts.

Many online businesses generate 10 percent to 30 percent of their sales through a network of affiliates who get payed a specified fee for the referral. Affiliate marketing was developed by CDNow in 1994 and popularized by Amazon, which now has more than 2 million affiliates. Top affiliates can make more than $1 million per year promoting everything from Amazon books to iPods to Dell computers.

There are four large affiliate networks -- Commission Junction, ShareASale, Google Affiliate network and LinkShare -- and several small to mid-sized affiliate programs. These networks recruit a large pool of affiliates and a number of businesses willing to offer the affiliates a percentage of sales or a finder's fee for a lead or the completion of a form on their website. The networks also acts as an escrow agent: They track the clicks and approved leads delivered by the affiliates, they provide detailed tracking results (see a sample report below) and they pay the affiliates so the advertiser only has to pay one amount at the end of the month vs. preparing hundreds of checks.

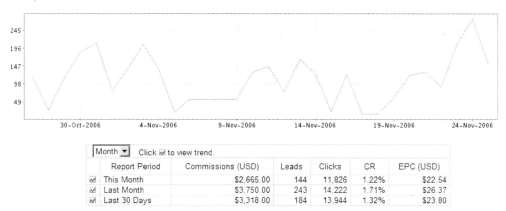

Affiliate marketing is a favorite of website marketers. Instead of paying Yahoo! or AOL to show banner ads in the hope that you can generate positive return on investment, with affiliate marketing you can set your finder's fee at $20 per sale and you know you have a locked in CPA (Cost Per Acquisition). You only pay when you generate a sale. The affiliates can become a virtual sales force generating profitable sales overnight.

A wide range of individuals and companies participate in affiliate marketing. There are four main types of affiliates:

1. Pay-Per-Click Search Engine Affiliates – These affiliates are experts in managing paid search engine campaigns. They invest in clicks on Google and the other search engines and send traffic to selected affiliate websites. They carefully track which programs are generating a positive return on their investment and they expand working programs and eliminate the poor performers.

2. Email Affiliates – This group of affiliates own large permission based email lists. The large affiliate networks do not allow SPAM, so legitimate lists with permission to mail are carefully regulated. These affiliates send offers to their lists and generate sales for their advertisers when consumers click on the email ads.

3. Content Websites – Highly trafficked sites can generate a large amount of clicks and sales for their advertisers. This is an area where natural search engine performance can generate tremendous return. If a site gets a lot of free traffic from the search engines, every affiliate sale generates a commission with no investment cost!

4. Coupon and Deal Affiliates – These affiliates offer discounts on products through unique coupon codes, and when a consumer makes a purchase using the code the affiliate who was issued the code gets a referral fee. These affiliates can drive a lot of traffic to their advertised sites and, in many cases, the advertiser will give the top performing affiliates a price that is better than the price on their own website. This is done to ensure that they are top performers

Ten Tips for Affiliate Marketing

Affiliates or 'publishers' are website operators, search engine marketers and/or email marketing specialists that market your website. And here's the best part. You get all of this marketing and promotion free, you only pay when a sale is made or a lead is generated. Think of them as a virtual sales force.

1.   Select a Solution. There are two ways to start an affiliate program: You can do it in-house or through an affiliate solutions provider. You'll need to accurately manage the tracking and reporting of your program, address technical issues and report on traffic and commissions, so if you don't have a large competent development team I recommend the solutions provider route.
The three biggest solutions providers are Commission Junction (who purchased BeFree) http://www.cj.com, Linkshare http://www.linkshare.com and Share A Sale www.shareasale.com .

2.   Your affiliate agreement is important. Draft a strong affiliate agreement and include two important decisions. Many programs are now restricting affiliates search keywords; the goal is to avoid bidding against your affiliates for top keywords. The other critical decision is how you will manage email policy. A No-Spam rule is critical to protect your brand image, and with the new CanSpam legislation in place it is critical to protect your company and your brand.

3.   Invite everyone, pick carefully. Add an "affiliate" link to your site's home page and include announcements about your affiliate program in newsletters and other customer communications. Review all affiliate applications carefully, have a look at their site and ensure they comply with your affiliate agreement.

4.   Make it easy to find and download creative. For website operators and emailers, great creative will improve clicks and conversions. Don't rely on the affiliate to develop the creative, develop great creative and make it easily available to your affiliate network. And, keep it fresh. Online creative burns out quickly so a steady stream of new banners and text ads will improve performance. Make sure your offers convert. Many affiliates will try a new product or service, but few will stick with it if they don't receive immediate rewards.

5.   Create Mini-Sites. Many successful marketers are developing several mini web site templates that affiliates can customize with logos and other information. These professionally designed sites convert better than home-grown designs and they allow your product or service to be presented in the best possible light.

6.   Assign a Full-Time Program Manager. A successful affiliate program requires full-time (or half-time) attention by one assigned manager. In the early days of the program, this manager will recruit affiliates and get creative and offers loaded and tested. As the program matures, the manager should nurture the relationships with affiliates, communicate new products and promotions, best performing creative etc.

7.   Embrace the 90:10 rule. In most businesses the Pareto Principle or 80:20 rule applies, that is 80 percent of your revenue will come from 20 percent of your customers. In most affiliate marketing programs, more than 90 percent of your revenue will come from under 10 percent of your affiliates. These "super affiliates" will be critical to the success of your program. Treat these affiliates like partners, communicate directly with them, listen carefully if they have complaints or suggestions and give them the best compensation agreements. Work hard with your solutions provider to recruit the best performing affiliates in other programs and offer your current affiliates an incentive to recruit other affiliates.

8.   Communication and Innovation. Communicate often with your affiliates, create an affiliate email newsletter and hold monthly affiliate webinars. Innovation will drive the program and innovative offers and contests will create interest and focus on your program vs. competitors.

9.   Visit the Shows and Forums. Stay in tune with latest trends and discussion through participation in affiliate forums such as www.abestweb.com . and http://www.affiliatemanager.net/index.shtml . Affiliate Summit is an amazing trade show and all of the major affiliate networks host their own events as well.

10.   Pay Frequently, Fairly and the Most. Affiliates are looking for revenue to fund their investment; they want to be paid fast and fairly. Pay for EVERY sale and compensate your affiliates for the lifetime value of a customer or compensate for all revenue from that customer. The top performers will seek out the top payers (per sale and top conversion percent), ensure that your program offers the best overall compensation deal in your business category.

Lead Generation (Lead Gen)

Lead Generation is similar to affiliate marketing: It takes some of the risk out of online advertising for the marketer by delivering qualified leads at a fixed rate. Leads are sent to the purchasing company as data files with the requested information such as name, telephone number email and lead criteria e.g.: this person is looking for a new mortgage, this person is shopping for a new car. You follow up on the leads by email or phone.

Lead Generation is often provided by companies that have large telemarketing teams calling people to generate enquiries or websites in niche industries with significant traffic to the sites. Lead Generation works for companies who want a fixed Cost Per Lead (CPL) but don't want to hire a large marketing or telemarketing team in house.

The Banner is Dead. Long Live the Banner!

Banner advertising was the main internet advertising tool until the growth of search engine marketing. Originally banners were static rectangular images presented at the top of web pages and the original banner was 468 pixels long and 60 pixels high.

A number of times over the past 10 years "experts" have declared that banner advertising was on its last legs. In the first dot-com boom (1997-2000) banner advertising costs escalated due to the increase in the number of brand advertisers buying banner space, increased demand allowed the advertisers to increase rates. Following the dot-com bust, the shine came off the banner for brand building and direct marketers (those of us who measure the effectiveness of each click) once again dominated the banner advertising space. By 2005 the brand advertisers had returned to the internet and CPM's (cost per 1000 impressions is a standard way websites charge for banner advertising) were increasing once again making positive return on investment (ROI) difficult for internet direct marketers. The recession of 2008/2009 has once again reduced demand for banners and it can be more cost effective to purchase banners with a ROI focus vs. branding.

Another factor limiting the effectiveness of the banner is a trend toward lower click-through rates. Click throughs are measured by the percentage of people who see a banner ad on a website divided by the percentage that click on it. Click-through rates have dropped from 3 percent to 4 percent in the 1990's to less than .05 percent in 2006. Despite reduced click-through rates, banners are still a mainstay of many profitable online advertising programs. Great creative and innovative use of technology can significantly increase click-through rates. As we explained in Chapter 1 test, test and test again to determine creative that works, placements that work and landing pages that deliver the trial, sign up or sale.

Banner Testing

Extensive testing is at the heart of all successful banner campaigns. You can test different banner creative, a range of banner sizes, and a variety of offers. Sophisticated technology for banners, often referred to as rich media, is also available. Some examples of rich media banners include flash banners that change colors and messages, expandable banners that enlarge when clicked on when you hold a mouse over them, interactive banners that can answer questions or let the users complete sign up forms, floating banners that move across the screen on top of the content, and video banners which display moving images and play audio.

eMail Marketing

There are two approaches to email marketing. Legal marketing to "opt-in" lists, lists generated when a consumer clicks on a box and says send me special promotions and email from your advertising partners, and illegal email marketing or "SPAM". Spammers develop lists by acquiring email addresses through contests and sign ups online or often by generating random emails to name combinations @ email providers.

Email marketing is generally inexpensive; however, doing quality email marketing is getting harder and harder. High quality opt-in lists are getting more expensive to use and it is very challenging to get the large email providers to allow the mail through to recipients. Large emailers often employ a full-time employee to manage the lists, removing people who request that they be unsubscribed from a list, dealing with email providers about complaints and blockage, and managing the technical side of clean emails.

Partner Marketing

Partner marketing takes place when two complimentary firms exchange text links or banners ads. For example, one site sells toys, the other site sells batteries, and each can promote the others products because the products work well together. Another example of partner marketing is when a firm provides content to another site in exchange for prominent links or banners on the site.

Paid Link Advertising and Text Link Exchanges

Over the past few years it has become common for highly ranked sites to receive polite emails from the webmasters of complimentary sites. These sites are questing links to their site or offering a link exchange – you link to me and I'll link to you. If both sites sell automobile accessories this can be beneficial to both because people who work on their cars might need tires and rims one month and interior parts the next.

Links are also very valuable for search engine marketing performance. Links coming to your site are more valuable than links trades or link exchanges, many websites were trading links just to boost their quantity of links and the search engines have discounted the value of one-for-one link trades.

Sites also offer links in exchange for one-time or monthly payments. This practice is frowned upon by the search engines, Google and the other engines are giving sites credit for links ***TO*** the site. Bought links negatively impact their ability to rate sites objectively and this tactic of link buying is considered less ethical when it comes to search engine optimization. However, a link is a link to a website and it will drive traffic if it is placed on a popular site.

Action Step 4-1 - Develop a Media Plan to Test Effectiveness

1. Set up a Google Pay-Per-Click campaign
2. Select keywords, develop ad copy and drive traffic to targeted landing pages
3. Test an offer that will generate an opt-in database (or drive sales if you have an eCommerce website)
4. Test other media to see if you can beat your Google Cost Per Acquisition (CPA)

Action Step 4-2 – Create an email Database

It is relatively easy to set up your customer and prospect database to regularly add leads and to mail eNewsletters and promotional email. Constant Contact, Vertical Response and other ESP's (email Service Providers) have inexpensively priced online database and email distribution software programs. Exact Target and Silverpop have slightly more expensive offerings and they will have a higher delivery rate for your programs.

Action Step 4-3 – Build Market Intelligence

There are a number of excellent products on the internet that will help you understand what your competitors are doing online. You should set up free accounts with the major affiliate networks (Commission Junction, LinkShare, ShareASale and the Google Affiliate Network) and monitor you competitor's affiliate programs. In addition, two websites provide excellent market intelligence: Compete.com has a number of web traffic reporting features and SpyFu.com reports on online advertising with a specialty in projecting Pay-Per-Click activity. Don't put too much stock in the free tools individually; instead, use them to paint a picture of competitive activity by compiling several reports.

Case Study – LifeScript.com

LifeScript.com is an online direct marketing company based in Mission Viejo, California. The company expanded from their core business of personalized vitamins to a product line that includes soy-based meal replacements and skin care products. LifeScript is a classical online direct marketer, they test dozens of offers, landing pages, every media property that they can uncover, and they are advanced search engine marketers.

One of the core marketing programs LifeScript developed was an eNewsletter called Healthy Advantage. The company discovered that they could acquire newsletter subscribers that turn into customers more cost effectively than they could acquire customers directly. The management team evolved the company into a profitable publisher with a talented and robust editorial department and they now generate more revenue form ads in the eNewsletters than from product sales. Along with the content development came a first-class business development team who aggressively sell advertising and marketing partnerships to reach LifeScript's targeted audience of millions of people interested in health and wellness.

Additional Information

"Winning Results with Google AdWords," Andrew Goodman explains how to succeed in the hypercompetitive world of Google Pay-Per-Click advertising.

On our Ten Golden Rules Internet Marketing Podcast we have featured several affiliate experts. In Episode 3 we interviewed Jeremy Palmer Author of "Quit Your Day Job", on Episode 8 we interviewed James Martell an affiliate entrepreneur and trainer and on Episode 41 we sat down with Shawn Collins, Author of "Successful Affiliate Marketing for Merchants" and co-founder of the popular Affiliate Summit Conference. http://podcast.tengoldenrules.com

Golden Rule #5 – Subscription Models Survive

Aside from eCommerce websites like Annie's Costumes, there are principally three business models that have worked on the internet. The advertising model, user generated content model and the subscription model.

The Advertising Model

The advertising model is the business approach taken by the large portals and select few leaders in every business category. Large portals such as Yahoo!, MSN and AOL have developed extensive websites with several engaging forms of content designed to keep the reader on the site to generate as many page views as possible. The more clicks, the more page views, the more banner advertising impressions generated.

For years, Yahoo! has been the No. 1 ranked website according to Alexa.com. Alexa ranks websites based on a combined measure of page views and visitors. The No. 2 ranked site on Alexa - Google, has more users but fewer page views, because Google users click off the site right away if they achieve their objective and deliver relevant search results. Yahoo! offers free web mail - and every email you view is a chance for them to present banner ads - they have extensive editorial content, free games, financial information, employment listings and dozens of other categories of information. They hold the No. 1 Alexa ranking by holding our interest on their site.

In the Alexa chart below, Yahoo! holds the No. 1 position in Alexa's Traffic Rank, followed by Google and upstart, YouTube. You can view Alexa's analysis of various websites at www.Alexa.com; Alexa provides detailed reporting for all websites in the top 100,000 positions in their ranking.

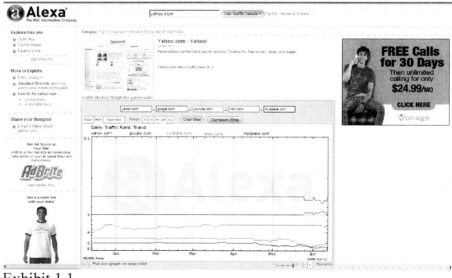

Exhibit 1.1

Leading specialty portals have evolved in many different interest niches. WebMD has become the leading medical portal (although some argue that Google is the first place most people go for personal medical research). iVillage owns a dominant position for women's eyeballs. Traditional media outlets, including CNN, have amassed leading news content on their portal-style websites. ESPN.com and CBSSportsline.com have developed a strong presence in online sports reporting.

The Advertising Model is generally profitable for a few large sites in each niche. One way some enterprising businesses have evolved the internet Ad Model is through the use of opt-in email newsletters. Businesses that can amass more than 100,000 subscribers, especially those with a demographic targeted by advertisers, can start selling advertising in email newsletters. Additionally, as readers open their email and click through, the host websites generates additional advertising "eyeballs." Regular, interesting emails are great reminders to visit your favorite sites. In addition to advertising in newsletters and on-site, email publishers will often send "endorsed" email advertising on behalf of their ad partners.

Social Media - User Generated Content

One of the most significant trends to evolve after the dot-com crash of 1999-2000 is the Social Media - User Generated Content (UGC) Website.

I attended a dinner at industry trade show Ad-Tech in San Francisco in 2003 and there was considerable buzz about a start-up website that allowed bands to create their own "space" on the website. The bands would promote upcoming concerts on the site, and fans of the bands could gather and share in the online community. Founded by Tom Anderson and Chris DeWolfe, MySpace became the first breakout website in this space as teens and young adults quickly adopted this site for their own self expression. In July of 2005, Rupert Murdoch's News Corporation purchased MySpace for $509 Million. MySpace has remained in its position as the largest online community, ranked No. 6 by Alexa, and slowly the site has been able to generate income, primarily though online advertising.

A student at Harvard University, Mark Zuckerberg founded another user generated content site, Facebook, in 2004. Membership was initially restricted to students of Harvard, and was expanded to all Ivy League schools by June. When Zuckerberg went to Palo Alto, California, for the summer, he never returned to finish his degree at Harvard. The following year Facebook opened its site to high school students and then to everyone in September of 2006. Despite limited advertising revenue, the privately owned site has an approximate valuation over $15 Billion!

Other UGC websites dominate in their niches including the incredible video website YouTube.com. Two friends, Chad Hurley and Steve Chen, founded YouTube after they couldn't find a website to upload videos from a party. The site was sold to Google for $1.65 Billion and it has become the No. 3 ranked Alexa site in the world!

CraigsList, founded by Craig Newmark who used to email his list of San Francisco area tech events to friends, has become the leading web classifieds directory. Digg is a site where users "dig" the most popular stories of the day. A top story on Digg will deliver 10,000 to 20,000 visitors to a website. Flickr, purchased by Yahoo! in 2005, is the top photo sharing website, and LinkedIn has become the leading business oriented social network.

The User Generated Content website is an extension of the Advertising Model from a business perspective. Although users create the content for the site, and they do most of the promotion for their individual pages, the site owners derive most of their revenue from advertising on users' pages.

Subscription Models Survive

The Advertising Model and the User Generated Content Model are both viable business models; however, they tend to favor the largest players in an industry. The Advertising Model requires significant volume of users and User Generated Content communities form where the largest mass of users hang out.

Subscription websites provide an excellent business opportunity for successful online entrepreneurs. Typically a subscription website offers a service or access to information in exchange for a monthly, quarterly or yearly subscription fee.

We typically pay a monthly fee for website access at home, and now on our mobile phones. We are often member of several monthly subscriptions for information or access to a set of information that is unique to our interests.

Classmates.com offers online social networking Web sites that enable users to locate and interact with acquaintances from high school, college, work and the military. The company serves more than 50 million registered accounts across its social networking websites, including 3.5 million pay accounts as of March 31, 2008. The model is simple: Classmates advertises throughout the internet with an invitation for you to look up your old high school or college friends. Users create a "profile" listing themselves in their appropriate school year and they are allowed to browse the class for free. If they want to contact their classmates or participate in online activities such as a school reunion they must upgrade their free profile to a paid membership.

The dating segment has embraced the subscription model. Users can create a profile on popular dating sites such as Date.com, Match.com and True.com, as with Classmates, you can view all of the attractive potential dates in your area for free, if you want to reach out to one of them you must become a paid member.

At eDiets.com we offered everyone who visited the site a free diet profile. Using the answers to a few questions such as your height, weight, age, medical conditions and food preferences we created a set of information about our program including a BMI (Body Mass Index) calculation and several charts defining how long it would take to achieve a healthy goal weight. In the free profile sign-up process, we asked for prospects email addresses and subscriptions to the free eNewsletter. The profile and eNewsletter were free, the customized online diet, including calorie specific meal plans, shopping lists, recipes and access to experts was a paid monthly subscription.

Netflix developed a sophisticated system to distribute DVD movies through the United States mail. The DVDs were shipped flat in special envelopes and movies were rented and returned in the same model as traditional brick and mortar rental stores. Netflix was close to going out of business when they switched to a monthly subscription model. With a monthly paid subscription, customers were shipped up to three movies, they can view as many movies as they want, subject to mailing one movie to Netflix and waiting for a new one to arrive in the mail. The subscription model was enthusiastically embraced by customers and Netflix changed the movie rental business, Blockbuster and other traditional retail rental locations moved towards the Netflix model.

Action Step 5-1

How can you take advantage of subscriptions in your business? Can you develop valuable industry information that your customers would pay to receive? If you're just entering the subscription business you can launch a free newsletter or blog and build your credibility. Hire freelance writers on websites such as Guru.com or eLance.com and develop content people will be anxiously awaiting each week or month.

Additional Learning

On the Ten Golden Rules Podcast Episode 4 we heard the story of successful subscription website Pandora.com, subsequently founder Tim Westergren has been featured on several international magazines covers and the company has become a breakout success. http://podcast.tengoldenrules.com

Golden Rule #6 Remember the 4 P's

For a costume store, Halloween season starts around mid-July. Orders start coming in from people living in other parts of the world and early birds start doing research for unique costumes and special requests. Also, costume inventory is coming in by the box and the team at Annie's Costumes gets busy stocking the warehouse. Once season starts, Shari doesn't get away for lunch until 3 or 4 in the afternoon, so we met close to the warehouse for a late bite. Sales were strong that year and our conversation centered on more traditional types of marketing. I explained the genesis of Golden Rule #6 Remember the 4 P's.

Internet Marketing is still marketing and the "Four P's of Marketing (Price, Place, Promotion, and Product) apply in this new online environment. The "Four P's" are very relevant in planning your marketing strategy and delivering your website to market.

Price

Price is one of the easy elements to test in online marketing. If you sell a product or service online, test different prices and evaluate the overall return on different price levels. (Retail style pricing generally works online $9.95 will work much better than $10.50 and $995 will outsell $1024 by a significant percentage. Test special offers (the classic TV direct marketing approach works ("buy the sharp cut knife and get a free orange juicer, but wait that's not all, we'll include a mini paring knife") Finding small niches, setting your price less than offline competition and testing a free trial that evolves into a paid subscription work well online.

As we learned with Golden Rule 1 – there are no pre-defined rules about what will work in the online environment since the internet customer sets the rules by reacting to the various options we offer. And she changes her mind frequently, so the rules today will change within days weeks or months – depending on your business. With online marketing there are few things we can test as easily, and with as much reliability as price. We can test price by varying the offer, the terms and the presentation of price.

The simplest way to test price is to present one price to half of your audience and another price to the second half. This is called A:B testing. We can do this simply with a Pay-Per-Click campaign or with email marketing. Create two offers and divide your list evenly and randomly. Make sure each list is equal to the other and don't send your existing customers one price and prospects the other price as this isn't an accurate test. A better idea is to divide your customer list into two and your prospect list into two and send half of each list Offer A and half Offer B.

Price testing applies for search engine marketing, email, websites, banners, etc. The winner is not the price with the most sales, but the price that generates the most revenue.

In the example below (Exhibit 6-1) for a product sold online and shipped to the customer we tested three price offers: Price A $19.95, Price B $24.95 and Price C $29.95 with free shipping included. Offer A generates the most purchases (74) and Offer C records the most top line revenue ($1,527.45), but Offer B returns the most Net revenue ($880.65).

	Price	Views	Purchases	% Sales	Revenue	Cost of Goods	Cost of Sales	Net Revenue
Price A	$19.95	100,000	74	0.07%	$1,476.30	$ 9.50	$ 703.00	$773.30
Price B	$24.95	100,000	57	0.06%	$1,422.15	$ 9.50	$ 541.50	$880.65
Price B	$29.95*	100,000	51	0.05%	$1,527.45	$ 13.50	$ 688.50	$838.95
	*includes free shipping							

Exhibit 6-1

Other factors to consider before deciding the winning offer include customer service costs, returns and credit card charge backs, and the cost of shipment preparation.

Once you have a winner, test again. Test to confirm the winner in different seasons or just to evaluate changes over time. And test different configurations of the offer, test different shipping costs and test a gift with purchase.

In Exhibit 6-2 below, we test three offers for a subscription product. The first offer sells the product for $195 for a one year subscription, Offer B is a monthly rate $19.95 and Offer C makes the subscription available for $4.95 per week. For this test and projected revenue analysis we need to project the retention, or the number of months the customer will continue to pay for his or her subscription. The yearly subscribers will renew at a lower rate than the monthly and weekly, so we projected that renewals would equal another 1/3 of a year, or four months. We projected the monthly customers would renew for seven months and the weekly customers would stay with the subscription for 19.5 weeks. In this example, Offer C delivers the most customers and the most revenue. Few companies will test an offer that lets the consumer out of their commitment so quickly. However, the online consumer often responds very positively to this type of offer. Give it a test to find out if it works for you!

	Price	Terms	Views	Purchases	% Sales	Projected Retention	Total Weeks	Revenue
Offer A	$195.00	For one Year	100,000	21	0.02%	1.4	65	$5,733.00
Offer B	$19.95	Per Month	100,000	47	0.05%	7	30	$6,563.55
Offer C	$4.95	Per Week	100,000	74	0.07%	19.5	19.5	$7,142.85

Exhibit 6-2

Place

In the retail world "place" is determined by your physical location(s). In packaged goods marketing, place can be influenced by shelf position and by positioning your products in advantageous places throughout a store such as end-aisle displays. In the online world, place can be influenced by your search engine marketing program, affiliate programs, partner marketing, and exclusive content deals.

Promotion

Promotion works well online. Contests, FREE with purchase and loyalty programs can all have a significant impact on click-through rates, conversion and overall online success.

Contests, long the staple of offline marketers from packaged goods to direct mail, can work well in your online marketing programs. A contest is a great tool to encourage customers to give you their email address and contact information, after all you will need a way to get in touch with the contest winner. In the contest entry form, ask the customer to opt-in to receive a newsletter or a special promotion and you now own a permission based opt-in email address for remarketing opportunities. Additionally, promoting a contest can be an encouragement for prospects to click on a banner, for site visitors to buy a product for a chance to win their purchase free, or a reason for a prospect to read more about a product or service when they come to a landing page.

A FREE gift with purchase is a traditional direct marketing practice that also works well online. An additional incentive can increase sales enough to pay for the cost of the incentive. One of the best tools you can use online is a free document that can be delivered as a PDF and the only cost is the development of the article as it can be delivered electronically at no cost online with a purchase. Another very strong offer is FREE shipping. I have seen this offer increase conversion, the percent of people who see an offer who act on that offer, by up to 30 percent!

Loyalty programs, or points programs, are very valuable when a customer can make multiple purchases at a site. So whether you're selling stamps, CD's or even computers, you can motivate the decision maker with a personal spiff of points towards incentives or gifts.

Product

On the internet your website is your "product". Think of the role of website manager as the role of product manager. How does the consumer react to your product? What is "new and improved?" What is your competitor doing that you could be doing better?

Action Step 6-1 – Price Testing

1. Brainstorm 5 different price options, and presentation of the price. If you sell a retail product, test the price, test the terms and the offer e.g.: do you charge $99 for one year, could you charge $10 per month, could you offer an option $10 a month or $99 pre-paid, how about $10 a month with one year pre-paid?
2. Create a projection in an excel spreadsheet – what level of sales will you require to beat out your existing offer? Are there other issues? Will you suffer from retention issues at a higher price, or possibly higher returns? Does your product have a higher perceived value at a higher price? Some products succeed with remarkably higher prices. Could you offer a greater service or guarantee at a higher price such as overnight shipping, free return shipping or 100 percent return guarantee.
3. Undertake testing "A vs. B" or "week vs. week," etc.

Case Study - Richard Parker
Founder and Chief Executive Officer
Diomo Corporation - The Business for Sale Buyer Resource Center™

Richard Parker launched an online extension to his business at www.Diomo.com on April 23, 2001. The company publishes and sells a number of "how to" guides on buying businesses. The company started out with one guide and has become very successful. They have expanded to eight other programs including a new version which they licensed to Donald Trump's company - Trump University.

Here are highlights from an interview with Richard from The Ten Golden Rules of Internet Marketing Podcast Episode 7.

There is no better product that you can sell on the internet than your own information product. It is proprietary, you own it, it is your knowledge and you can build on that knowledge to become an expert in your field. If you sell a "me too" widget, you are faced with a ton of potential competition since anybody else can sell a similar or better widget. The creation of information products is a great business model for a number of reasons: They are inexpensive to create, cost-effective to manufacture especially if someone downloads the book as a PDF, you do not need a lot of infrastructure to support it, you can outsource nearly every function, fulfillment houses eliminate any inventory requirements, you do not have any receivables and once you set it up properly, the business operates 24/7/365.

We started out with one guide, and we did not even know if we would sell a single copy. Although I have owned 10 businesses, this model is the greatest. In addition to helping thousands of people in over 80 countries now, I have the best time because I make money while I sleep. When I wake up in the morning and I see the orders, next to seeing my kids it is the biggest thrill I have each day. The company is now at the point where I can work the business when I want, if I want, and from any place. It is really on auto pilot.

There are two strategies you can follow with an online business. You can either take the shotgun approach by trying to be all things to all people, or, you can use a laser beam approach and be highly focused. I have learned that niche products with built-in demand, really separates your online business from the competition. This is the laser beam strategy. I used to try to address every potential prospect's needs and wants but then I stumbled upon another great opportunity. We sent a survey to everyone who bought the guides and we asked people why did you buy our product and what was their biggest concern about buying a business? Seventy-six percent of the people said their biggest worry was buying the right business. Overnight, we changed all of the copy and focused on the theme of how to buy the right business and avoid buying the wrong business. We focused on the hot buttons of the majority of people, and our conversion rates went up by 25 percent overnight.

We naturally optimized the site -- I call it accidental optimization. I started writing a ton of articles on buying a business because I wanted people to stick on my website. I started posting the articles on the site, and three wonderful things happened. First, we started getting increased rankings and traffic. Second, when people came to the site and read these articles, I believe they began to think: "If I get this kind of content for free I can't wait to see what I'll get with the guide that costs money." Third, I went to everybody in my industry; even my competitors, knowing they are all looking for content and I offered the articles to them for free -- I just asked them to include a link-rich byline back to our site. I set the articles up with a byline top and bottom with my name and a link to my site. Now I have thousands of these articles all over the internet linking to my website and the content continues to push our rankings. We are on page one of Google for over 90 percent of the main keywords in our industry.

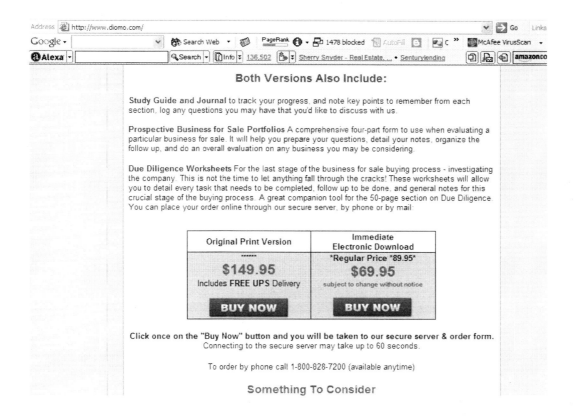

Something To Consider

Golden Rule #7 Use the Right Tactic

There is no 'silver bullet'

There is no "silver bullet" in internet marketing. There are no guarantees for success and no sure-fire success strategies.

However, through the application of the Ten Golden Rules, the core strategies and approaches to internet marketing, and lots of testing, you can significantly increase your chances of success by applying the right tactic for the appropriate objective.

Certain Tactics for Certain Objectives

Certain tactics apply for certain objectives, for example in addition to Pay-Per-Click, natural search engine optimization and affiliate marketing covered in previous chapters, email and newsletter marketing, as well as banner ads, are often good tactics to acquire new customers.

Paid Search Engine Marketing

Paid Search Engine Marketing or PPC (Pay-Per-Click) search engine marketing ads are the small ads that appear on the top of a search or on the right hand side of an internet search. Below are two examples of Pay-Per-Click ads for Ten Golden Rules. The first ad appears on a Google search for the keyword term "internet marketing consultants". The right side, the Pay-Per-Click area of Google is identified by the term "Sponsored Links" circled in the example below (Image 7-1). The ad for Ten Golden Rules appears in the fourth position, below three other advertisers. As with all online advertising, you must test different ad positions and different ad copy to determine which ads yield the best results, but as a general rule position three to six will yield the best results. In many categories, advertisers will over bid to guarantee position 1 or 2, this is often driven by CEO ego "I want my ad first regardless of the cost" and these ad positions will not yield positive Return on Investment (ROI).

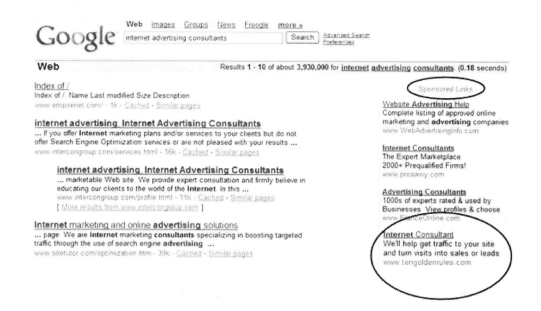

When prospects click on this ad, Ten Golden Rules will be charged $0.90 based on a Current Maximum CPC (Cost Per Click) of $0.90 in the Google AdWords report below. Google, Yahoo!, Bing/MSN and other smaller search engines provide detailed tools and reports for the advertiser to manage their Pay-Per-Click campaign.

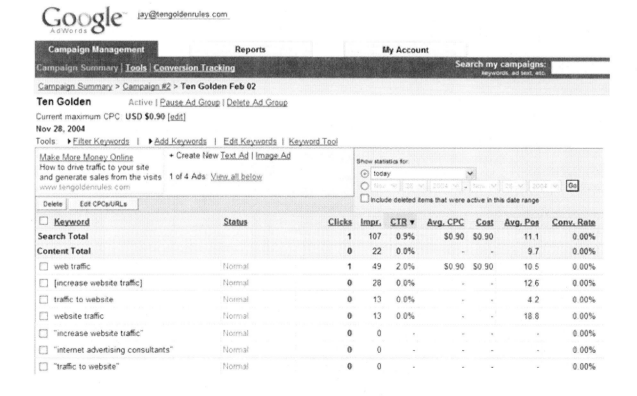

Email Marketing

Email marketing is very similar to direct marketing. Lists of highly defined target individuals are available for rental or purchase by several reputable companies. Your most profitable email programs target your existing customers, or your "house list."

There are five main things that will contribute to the success of an email marketing campaign: **Lists, Subject Lines, Offer, Creative and Landing Pages.**

Lists

Your lists will dramatically affect the results of your campaign. Professional email list companies build opt-in lists of consumers and businesses who have allowed the use of their email address for future email offers and messages. The list companies add as many pieces of information as possible to the data files so that you can select leads based on this information. For example, you can target males, or females, you can target by age and by region. Additionally, many lists have detailed "interest" information, so you can target everything from bird lovers to boat enthusiasts.

Subject Lines and From Lines

The second factor that will affect your campaign success is the subject line and from line. With today's crowded email inboxes, often the difference between a profitable campaign and a failure is what they see at first glace. Think of your own inbox, how many emails do you delete without even looking at the content?

The subject line can actually be more important than the ad itself, yet often they are written minutes before the email goes out. The subject line acts like the headline of an ad or a billboard, it can gain the interest of the reader and interest him or her to read more.

You should state the primary purpose of the message and phrase it as a benefit for the reader. It is often beneficial to start the subject line with a verb.

The first 40 characters are very important as most web-based email systems only display 40 characters; and, the maximum length should be no more than 50 characters.

It is tempting to use words like FREE in the subject line, however, most filters will block these messages from getting through. Also avoid the use of dollar signs, hyphens and multiple periods.

The from line should identify the company or sender as accurately as possible, the more familiar the reader is with your name or company, the better. In some instances the list renter might include their company name to warm up the message for you.

The main role of the subject line is to get the user to look at the email.

Ten Tips for eMail Campaigns

1. The 40:40:20 rule from direct marketing is applicable to email. Forty percent of your success will come from your offer (test, test, test!), 40 percent from your lists (more testing) and 20 percent of your success from your creative design and testing.

2. Test different subject lines, this is the first opportunity to interest the prospect.

3. Keep subject lines short (40 characters are optimal), start with a compelling verb, state the one primary purpose of the message.

4. Avoid the use of words like free, win, contest, Viagra and naked -- they will get caught in the SPAM filters.

5. Design your email with the Outlook preview pane in mind. Make sure the top portion of the email carries your key message to ensure clicks from people previewing that portion of the image.

6. Design your email to read top to bottom and left to right.

7. A picture is worth a thousand words. Show an aspirational image, top left on the banner to immediately capture the reader's attention.

8. Place your call-to-action in the bottom right portion of the email "above the fold" which means that it is visible on a normal computer screen and doesn't require scrolling. Use a colored button that looks obviously clickable. A good example would be the Windows 2003 buttons that people would find familiar.

9. Use multiple calls to action <u>Click here to start now</u>, <u>START NOW</u>, <u>Click to begin!</u> And test different interaction devises a choice of buttons to click on or a scroll down option engages your prospect and gets the click.

10. Send your clicks to specific relevant landing pages NOT to your home page. If someone clicks on the offer take them to a page where they can buy that product or service, if they click on read more go to a relevant information page.

Offer

The offer will be critical to success of the campaign. Is it relevant to the receiver? Is this a unique and rich offer worthy of their interests? Is it something better than other offers they've seen before and is there a special benefit for dealing with this company or ordering online? Is there an incentive for ordering right away?

Creative

The creative must compel the viewer to click for more information or to order online. Most email creative takes the form of a one page ad and includes a great headline, a strong graphic and a call to action in the bottom right hand section of the ad (people read left to right and top to bottom and their eyes end up at the bottom right).

Particular attention should be paid to the top portion of the ad creative. In Microsoft Outlook the preview screen will show the top of the ad and this gives you another chance to catch the attention of the prospect.

The main role of your email creative is to get the user to click through to the website.

Landing Page

If your email was sent to a live email address, and it succeeds in getting past the filters, and the consumer clicks on the subject line and clicks on the ad it is valuable to match the messaging of the ad with the messaging on the landing page. A landing page can be any page on a website that you direct users to visit.

If you are advertising a special offer for Harry Potter Costumes, for example, but you direct the user to your home page and they have to search through your site to find the offer, there is a good chance they'll get lost, frustrated or start to lose interest. They will either close the window immediately, or if they are really intrigued by the offer they will start searching. However, if they can't locate the offer relatively quickly their interest will likely pass and they will leave your site.

eNewsletters

Email newsletters are a critical part of most successful online marketing campaigns. This tactic has many benefits:

- The "Sign Up For a FREE Newsletter" offer is a strong UVP (see Chapter 3 Unique Value Proposition) a reason for people to give you their email address and permission to email them in the future. This permission allows you to include offers and special deals in the emails that will build your business.

- It is beneficial to allow site visitors to see previous newsletter articles on your website. This will increase sign-up rates to your newsletter.

- An eNewsletter with valuable information will be opened regularly by your customers and prospects it will keep you top of mind.

- If the content is really good, your customers and prospects will give you the best recommendation in marketing, a word-of-mouth referral to a friend, associate or co-worker. Make it easy for them to refer your eNewsletter and put a "Forward this Article" link on your newsletter stories.

- Newsletters are often printed and stored in files or stored in online files for future reference. Next time your prospect (or one of their friends) is looking for your products and services you are top of mind and they have an easy way to find you!

Newsletter articles are a tremendous way to add content to your website. Each week or month when you publish your newsletter, add the articles to your site as unique search engine optimized web pages. Select 2-3 unique keyword phrases and use those phrases 2-3 times in the article.

Online Advertising

Banners and links on websites play a dual role of building brand awareness and driving measurable sales results. This tactic is a good way to build broad reach as you can advertise on sites to reach new prospects.

Contrary to popular belief, banners do work.

Online advertising expenditure is at an all time high and I have worked on a number of very, profitable banner campaigns. However, bad banners will not achieve your objectives. Where possible use rich media, banners that feature movement or changing words or pictures, this tactic achieves up to three times the click through rates of static banners.

Action Step 7-1

If you haven't tested a Pay-Per-Click search campaign, what are you waiting for? For as little as $5 you can set up a Google campaign today. You will only pay for clicks on your ads so this type of advertising is very measurable and it can provide a direct return on your investment.

Action Step 7-2

Do you have an eNewsletter program? If not you should make this a priority, everyone from retailers to B2B marketers can benefit from a newsletter campaign. Offer your free eNewsletter on your website and promote it through your sales force and call center.

Golden Rule # 8 Trust is Golden

Consumers Look for Security Indicators

Over the past five years, consumers have become more and more trusting of the internet. Luddites (someone opposed to technology and progress) are becoming very rare and rarely do you hear someone say, "I'll never put my credit card into the computer."

Consumers have improved confidence in internet security and the reliability of shipping and fulfillment; however, consumers don't willingly spend money on every website. There are a number of strategies web marketers should employ to improve the trust consumers have on their eCommerce and non-eCommerce websites.

Consumers look for the indicators of secure eCommerce. When a site is secure, the website address changes form http:// to https:// signifying a secure connection. A lock or other indication of a secured site will appear, normally on the bottom right hand side of the site (See example below).

Additionally, the inclusion of recognizable security logos such as the Better Business Bureau Reliability Program and Verified by Visa can build online sales by as much as 40 percent!

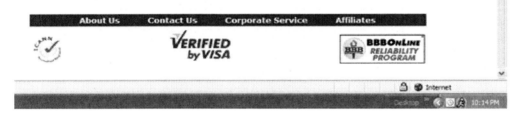

The inclusion of industry accreditation (such as the ICANN logo in the example above), a logo or mark that would be recognized by people from a specific field can improve site results. In one case earlier in my career we added the logo of a widely recognized national association to the web site landing page and credit card information page and sales increased an incredible 17 percent. This was the single most successful test for this website in over one year.

Do Not Violate CAN-SPAM
Controlling the Assault of Non-Solicited Pornography and Marketing Act of 2003

In December of 2003, United States President George W. Bush signed the CAN-SPAM Act "Controlling the Assault of Non-Solicited Pornography and Marketing Act of 2003" into law. Full text of the law is available at: http://www.ftc.gov/spam

In November of 2004, one of the first major SPAM prosecutions was announced with a North Carolina man, Jeremy Jaynes, convicted by a jury of three felony counts of sending unsolicited bulk e-mail. Jaynes was reported to have more than 100 million email addresses and used a program called Robomail to send out more than 10,000 unwanted email addresses in a 24 hour period. To make matters worse, he was selling products that didn't exist!

Here are the major points of CAN-SPAM Act to help keep you away from the long arm of the law. Here's a rundown of the law's main provisions:

- It bans false or misleading header information. Your email's "From," "To," and routing information – including the originating domain name and email address – must be accurate and identify the person who initiated the email.

- It prohibits deceptive subject lines. The subject line cannot mislead the recipient about the contents or subject matter of the message.

- It requires that your email give recipients an opt-out method. You must provide a return email address or another internet-based response mechanism that allows a recipient to ask you not to send future email messages to that email address, and you must honor the requests. You may create a "menu" of choices to allow a recipient to opt out of certain types of messages, but you must include the option to end any commercial messages from the sender.

- Any opt-out mechanism you offer must be able to process opt-out requests for at least 30 days after you send your commercial email. When you receive an opt-out request, the law gives you 10 business days to stop sending email to the requestor's email address. You cannot help another entity send email to that address, or have another entity send email on your behalf to that address. Finally, it's illegal for you to sell or transfer the email addresses of people who choose not to receive your email, even in the form of a mailing list, unless you transfer the addresses so another entity can comply with the law.

- It requires that commercial email be identified as an advertisement and include the sender's valid physical postal address. Your message must contain clear and conspicuous notice that the message is an advertisement or solicitation and that the recipient can opt out of receiving more commercial email from you. It also must include your valid physical postal address.

Study Security Safeguards

One of the greatest risks to your online reputation is the threat of hackers, internet scoundrels who break into your internet website and perform unwanted or illegal actions.

One of the favorite practices of SPAMMERS is to hack into the server of an unsuspecting website and send SPAM email from the websites' email addresses. This can violate the trust you have with your customers and get your site blacklisted with internet services providers (ISP's). Blacklists are lists that the ISP's compile of companies that send unwanted or reported SPAM. When their customers complain about an unusually high percentage of emails form one sender, the sender is banned from the system and none of their emails will get through until the offending website petitions the ISP to get off the blacklist.

Privacy Policy Prominent

Website visitors will look for your Privacy Policy, in many cases it is sufficient for them to see a link to your privacy policy and information capture on online forms will increase.

The Importance of Web Site Design

The Stanford University Persuasive Technology Lab conducted a study on consumer's perceptions of website credibility http://credibility.stanford.edu. 2,684 people evaluated live web sites in 10 content categories including eCommerce, entertainment, finance, health, news, nonprofit, opinion or review, search engines, sports, and travel. A total of 100 sites were assessed.

The study found that when people assessed a web site's credibility they did not use rigorous criteria. The data showed that the average consumer paid far more attention to the superficial aspects of a site, such as visual cues, than to its content. For example, nearly half of all consumers (or 46.1 percent) in the study assessed the credibility of sites based in part on the appeal of the overall visual design of a site, including layout, typography, font size and color schemes.

28.5 percent of consumers commented on the organization of the site's information, and 25.1 percent how well or poorly the information fit together. Consumers commented on how hard it was to navigate the site to find things of interest, sites that were easy to navigate were seen as being more credible.

The site's perceived motive was an important factor for 15.5 percent of study participants. Web sites lost credibility when the only purpose of a site seemed to be selling things or getting money from users. In other cases, web sites won credibility by conveying motives that people found to be admirable. This underlines the importance of a UVP on a web site (Unique Value Proposition - Chapter 3). Include one or more free tools that consumers can use, free newsletters or free white papers, your site will be perceived as more credible.

Action Step 8-1

1. Visit any areas of your site where you are asking consumers to enter personal information and credit cards. Is the page secure (https) and displaying a lock or other proof of a secure site? Are there marks of credibility such as Better Business Bureau, Trust-e or industry Association logos. What can you do to improve your website to improve consumer response and conversion?

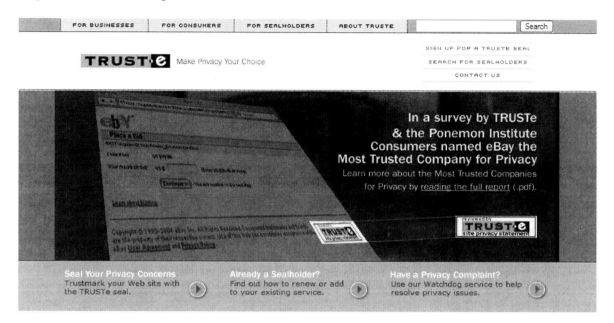

Action Step 8-2 Are you SPAM compliant?

Are your email policies SPAM compliant? Visit the website http://www.ftc.gov/bcp/conline/edcams/spam/business.htm to ensure you are not in violation of Federal law.

Action Step 8-3 Does your web design convey a sense of credibility and trust?

- Is your website professional looking?
- Is it easy to navigate?

Does it offer free tools and advice or is it sell, sell, sell? If you haven't confirmed these elements with consumers you might want to conduct some formal or informal consumer research to ensure that your website is conveying a sense of credibility and trust with consumers.

Golden Rule # 9 The Best Never Rest

Never Settle

Great online marketers are constantly testing and never settling for their current results.

It is easy to test things online: Change a button, test an offer, change a photo, substitute a testimonial for a product shot, test new search keywords, and try new creative for your email campaign.

Shari and the team at Annie's Costumes have become passionate about testing new technologies and new ways to generate traffic to their website. In recent years we have developed the following projects, and many more: blogs, viral games, trivia contests, photo contests, YouTube videos and we built a store in the leading virtual world Second Life. Shari is also active on Facebook where the company has a Facebook page and she is popular on Twitter.

Innovation and evolution drives business success. Tony Robbins coined the term 'CANEI' which stands for Constant and Never-Ending Improvement. Robbins was looking for an American term similar to the Japanese term Kaizan (Kai = change Zen = Good, change is good), both terms refer to the constant improvement process that propels personal development and business success.

This approach to constant improvement is especially valuable online. It is easy and inexpensive to test online and it is easy to gather quantifiable results to measure the success of tests. Many times changing the website improves performance just because it is different and fresh.

Test, Measure Results and Re-test

Most important, measure the results. Here are some of the components to test and measure:

<u>On a Website</u>

- Click through rates (percent of site visitors to click on an offer or ad)
- Percent completed forms (percent of site visitors to request information, complete an application or a free profile)
- Sales percent (percent of site visitors that make a purchase online)
- Newsletter subscriptions (percent of visitors that ask for a free email newsletter)
- Percent downloading a white paper or viewing an article
- Bounce rate (Percent who see only one page on your site and exit)
- Exit rate per page (Percent who exit from each page on your site)

For eMail or Advertising Campaigns

- Test different creative
- Test rich media creative
- Test new landing pages specific to the ad or email
- Test new offers

For Paid Search Campaigns (PPC)

- Test new keywords
- Test bid rates and ad position
- Test new ad copy that matches the keywords you are targeting
- Test new landing pages
- Test a new PPC Search company in addition to Google, Yahoo and Bing/MSN and smaller search engines such as ASK.com, 7Search, MIV and FindWhat

For Natural Search Engine Marketing (SEO)

- Regularly add new web pages optimized for SEO
- Add new sections to your website
- Make sure you have a site map link on every page
- Launch a weekly or monthly eNewsletter and add the optimized articles to your website
- Try a link building campaign

Website Analytics

There are several excellent website analytics programs that will tell you how many visitors you had to your site in a defined time period. You can also determine where those visits came from, how many people "bounced" or left your site after viewing only one page, you will determine what keyword people searched to find your site, where did they leave your site - did they exit when they came to the credit card page?

Google Analytics is a free analytics program that offers most of the key functionality that the paid analytics programs offer. For a small business, adding Google analytics code to your site will provide more information than you will have time to analyze.

We add Google Analytics code to all of our client's websites, we highly recommend it.

Below is an example of the first page of a Google Analytics report. The report shows us traffic to the site, where the traffic comes from and there are extensive links to the other information and reporting tools.

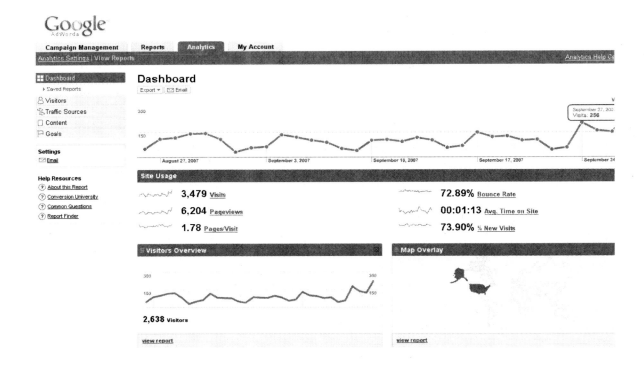

Develop a Top Ten Priority List

Most of the organizations we work with in our consulting practice develop a Top Ten Priority List for online tests and development projects.

We prioritize the tests that we think will deliver the biggest benefit. Using the priority list, the marketing and development teams can work together to create the tests and get them up online. This system is very effective as everyone knows what to focus on and it is a very powerful way to focus the efforts of the organization in the right direction.

It Doesn't Have To Be Perfect!

The most important part of a testing strategy is velocity and frequency. Test early and often. Don't wait to build every component of a back-end delivery system before you test something. For example, if you want to test a different price, change the price on screen and bill the credit cards manually. If the test is a success you can build the back-end program to change price points later.

Ten Tips for Generating Revenue from Website Traffic

Selling directly to customers and generating leads for your business are not the only ways to generate revenue online. There are many ways you can profit from the traffic to your website. Here are ten tips to generate revenue from the existing visits to your web site.

1. <u>Join Relevant Affiliate Programs</u>

Have you ever been on a website and seen a small add that says "Buy this book on Amazon.com?" There is a good chance that ad was placed by an Amazon affiliate. An affiliate is paid a "finders fee" for customers they send to a website. You can generate revenue by referring people to sites with products or services that interest your website visitors. For more information visit the largest affiliate networks http://www.cj.com or http://www.linkshare.com www.ShareASale.com or click the 'affiliate' link on any major website.

2. <u>Sell Advertising on Your Site</u>

You can offer advertising space to advertisers with complimentary products. Charge them by the click or perhaps strike a deal where they pay you for every customer they acquire.

3. <u>Increase Sales 5 percent to 15 percent with an Exit Pop-up</u>

Most of us dislike pop-up ads, but if someone is leaving your site without purchasing anything, isn't it worth one more chance to catch their attention? Exit pop-up ads can generate 5 percent to 15 percent of daily sales for most websites.

4. <u>Sell Sponsored Content Areas</u>

In many industries, companies would be willing to provide content (articles, online tools and functionality) in exchange for recognition and a link to their website. For example on MSN, ESPN provides sports information and MSNBC provides financial news.

5. <u>Sell 'Opt-in' Traffic in the Sales Funnel</u>

Many companies will pay for names and email addresses of people who have opted to receive information and special offers. For example, magazine subscription companies will pay a finders fee for every person that agrees to receive a free trial of a publication.

6. <u>Sell Relevant or Complimentary Products (removed period)</u>

If you sell toys, offer to ship the required batteries with the toy for a special price. If you sell books, offer a book mark or book light with the purchase.

7. <u>Sell Your Exit Traffic</u>

When a customer clicks on the little "x" at the top right hand corner of your site, don't despair, send her to a complimentary website. Utilize an affiliate code or arrange for a CPA (Cost Per Acquisition) or CPL (Cost Per Lead) reward for customers that the destination site is able to convert.

8. <u>Create a "For Sale" or "Coming Soon" Parking Page (removed period)</u>

If you own domain names that don't yet have websites designed, you can create a page to offer the domain name for sale, or to let customers know it is in development and "coming soon." There are a number of programs that allow you to run links and ads on these pages to generate revenue.

9. Partner with www.WebLoyalty.com

Give your customers premium savings and services, making your site a more attractive for the consumer. Programs and services webloyalty.com offers include travel discounts, shopping savings, entertainment discounts and home computer protection.

10. Run Google and Yahoo! Ads on Your Site

Google AdSense matches ads to your site's content, and you earn money whenever your visitors click on them. For example if you had a costume website your AdSense ads would show ads for people targeting costume keywords.

Action Step 9-1

1. Develop a Top Ten Priority list and start testing!

Additional Learning

"Analytics an Hour a Day," Google Analytics Evangelist Avinash Kaushik shows you how to make website Analytics a powerful tool.

Golden Rule #10 Lead the Trends

Unlike the offline world, the internet market will change every six months, or sooner. To succeed in online marketing you must stay ahead of the curve and constantly test new strategies and tactics.

Since we may have identified new trends by the time you read this, please visit our website at www.TenGoldenRules.com/book we'll keep the trends updated. We also have a free blog with trends and commentary that is up-to-the-minute and we produce The Ten Golden Rules of Internet Marketing Podcast with expert interviews and great content from the Ten Golden Rules team. Find it all at www.TenGoldenRules.com .

Remember Pop-Up Ads?

Remember pop-up ads? These were the coolest things when we first encountered them. You would be on a technology website looking at a new digital camera and up popped an ad to win a digital camera, "cool" we thought and we clicked on the ad.

Soon it wasn't cool at all. We were getting dozens of pop ups every time we went online. We quickly learned that these were ads and we started adding pop-up blockers to our security software, soon thereafter our Internet Service Providers (ISP's), the companies we use to give us internet access, were blocking pop ups for us and in no time (about six to 12 months) pop ups were, for the most part, a thing of the past.

As a marketer, pop ups were one of the most powerful tools in the history of online advertising. Sold as "contextual ads" and popularized by a company called Gator (Gator has since changed their name to Claria) often the ads were "popped-up" when a web surfer went to a web page and spyware read a target keyword on the page. This made the ads appropriate to the content or "context" on the page, very targeted and very effective. Many Gator Ads even popped up on competitor's web pages.

Pop ups were getting incredible click-through rates, often more than 40 percent! As a marketer, if you found out about this tactic early on, optimized your keyword buys, tested creative and landing pages you were able to make tremendous profit on your pop-up campaigns. If you decided to test pop ups after they had been out for six or eight months they likely didn't generate positive return on your investment and likely cast a negative shadow on your brand.

This is not a recommendation for pop ups or Gator Ads. This is an example of the speed of the internet and the importance of staying on top of the leading trends. In internet marketing, new opportunities come in, get hot, then they get tired or too competitive and they stop working. Occasionally, the old trends come back and start working again. To succeed, staying on top of the hot trends is imperative.

"How Can I Stay on the Leading Edge?"

So, you might ask "How do I stay on top of the leading trends in Internet Marketing?"

Research, Read, Learn, Surf, Study, Subscribe to Blogs and Podcasts, Ask Questions, Network. Look at the leaders -- make it a practice to visit the best online marketers such as Amazon, Dell and the online leaders in your industry or category. Live online. Shop online. Become an avid online practitioner and adapt learning from sites that you like. Did an email catch your eye? How can you apply their subject line or landing page for your business? Did you buy a trip online? How did the search function work, what was the offer that convinced you to buy? How can you apply the learning?

The Ten Leading Trends in Online Marketing

Here are the ten leading trends (at the time of writing) that will help you get ahead in online marketing. Please visit www.TenGoldenRules.com/book for updated versions of the Ten Leading Trends in Online Marketing.

1. **Micro Marketing**

Marketing through small intimate connections with customers is becoming an effective trend. Twitter.com is a website where people and companies can follow each others 'tweets,' short messages up to 140 characters that people are calling micro blogging. Originally the site asked the question "What are you doing?" but user have found many different uses. News sites such as CNN are sending out breaking news tweets and the company Woot.com sends a tweet with one specially priced product that they sell each day. Individuals subscribe to dozens or hundreds of blogs and receive notifications on their cell phones and computers, and inventive companies are communicating with opt-in customers on their cell phones using text messaging.

2. **Customer Service is the New Marketing**

With a significant increase in the power of consumer journalism a major part of the marketing function is moving to customer service departments. 'CS' departments are reaching out to bloggers and online message boards to deal with unhappy customers before situations and frustrations escalate. Dell Computers has gone from extremely negative online publicity to take an active participatory role in the online community.

3. **Podcasts**

The "Tipping Point" for me with podcasts was when I found a couple of great marketing podcasts. Immediately I was searching Google and iTunes for more of this great FREE content. I believe this is the most explosive exciting thing happening in the digital world. I can learn amazing things and be entertained by the brightest minds in the areas I am most passionate about. I can shift learning time, now I don't have to be able to read a book or a computer to learn, I'm can learn cutting edge information while I'm stuck in traffic, on a treadmill at the gym, in line at the bank or walking my dog.

We love podcasts so much that we recently launched the Ten Golden Rules of Internet Marketing Podcast; and, it is free on our website and iTunes.

I am a regular listener to search Guru Danny Sullivan's Daily Search Cast, Shel Holtz and Neville Hobson's For Immediate Release a New Media PR Podcast, Affiliate Summit's Shawn Collins and Lisa Picarille from Revenue Magazine do a great Affiliate Podcast called That Affiliate Thing, Mitch Joel does the amazing Six Pixels of Separation and Joe Jaffe is Jaffe Juice. I am also enjoying a music podcast called Electronic Groove featuring one hour mixes by DJ's from around the world, and I love Grapevine, Don Cherry's hockey podcast.

4. Virtual Worlds

Second Life is a virtual world developed by a company called Linden Labs. In Second Life you can create your own 'avatar' and travel through virtual islands. You can buy virtual land from Linden Labs with a currency that can be exchanged for US dollars. You hold virtual meetings and events and purchase items for your avatar and your virtual buildings. Anshe Chung a Second Life real developer has declared herself the first person to become a real world US dollar millionaire through transactions made in Second Life. If you're an internet marketer you must check it out http://www.Secondlife.com . Also watch Club Penguin "Second Life" for children, purchased by Disney for $310 Million and World of Warcraft.

5. Local

Until recently one of the restrictions of paid search engine marketing and banner advertising had been the ability to market in a specific geographic region. Several exciting new technologies now make it practical and affordable for Vinny's Pizza to compete in the online space. Google, Yahoo! and Bing/MSN all have local search tools that have recently emerged from their labs and DoubleClick's Dart for Advertisers gives you the ability to target banner ads to specified local geography. Blended, or Universal, search results often show maps results at the top of the main search engine results and more and more consumers are searching for businesses and information using the maps function on search engines and cell phones. Below is an example of a search using Google Local for a shoe repair in Boca Raton, Florida.

6. Social Media

The major trend driving the growth of social Media sites is user generated content - web pages created and promoted by users not by website owners. MySpace.com is the largest social network, YouTube.com is barely four years old and it is ranked No. 3 in the world by Alexa behind just Yahoo! and Google! CraigsList.com is a site featuring mostly free listings of rentals and job opportunities, it is displacing classified advertising in newspapers, FaceBook.com has a $15 Billion valuation, Flickr a photo sharing site is in the top 40 sites on Alexa, and Digg.com allows its 1,000,000 visitors a day to vote for top news stories and has been called 'the new New York Times'.

7. Website Usability

A lot of online marketers have realized they are pretty good at driving traffic to the site. One of the top trends in our consulting business is to improve the user experience and conversion percentage once a visitor comes to a website.

Web site usability is a simple thing. As I mentioned earlier, Steve Krug in his great book on the topic of usability "Don't Make Me Think" explains that the most important thing when designing a website is to make it easy to figure out. It should be obvious to the user what the site is all about, and where to click to find what they're looking for.

Many companies haven't updated their website since they developed it in 1999 or 2000 and more and more of them are focusing on user needs and cutting out the clutter that clogs most old school sites. Smart sites are now delivering a laser-like focus on user goals and making it easy for customers to find what they want in two to three clicks.

Certain web design standards are becoming the "convention" and web surfers know to look for these elements:

- Web site logo goes on the top left corner and when clicked while on secondary pages throughout the site, it returns users to the home page
- The home page should make it clear what the site offers and how to use it. Often a clear tagline can explain what the site is all about, if not, a short paragraph of copy at the very top should accomplish this objective.
- Navigation (links to take you around ~~the~~ a site) should be on the left side or across the top
- Twenty percent to 30 percent of web surfers prefer to search when they come to a site. The top right corner is becoming a standard placement for the search box. The box should be big and white and beside it the word search should be clearly readable.
- As users travel through the site, it should be clear what section they are in, where they came from and how to get back to the home page from where they are.
- Make it easy for your internal team to update the website on a regular basis so there is a reason for prospects to come back again and again. One great way to accomplish this is to put a section on the home page to feature a newsletter article. Each month (week or day) you can feature an article from your newsletter. This achieves two objectives, it keeps the site fresh and it promotes sign up for your newsletter which gives you permission to re-market to your prospects and keeps you top-of-mind.
- Test the site for usability. This can be as simple as watching friends, family and employees navigate the website, or it can be accomplished with professional web site usability studies. User testing is a must for all new web projects.

8. Email is Back!

Many internet strategies seem to fall out of style and return with a flair. One of these to come back to focus is email. With the rush of viruses and the growth of SPAM many consumers were afraid to open emails from anyone they didn't know. With CAN-SPAM 2003 regulations and improved virus spotting software we seem to be more trusting of email. This means that open rates are increasing and programs are becoming more and more successful. Your best list is always your own customer list. Sending your customers a special offer or chance to buy gifts or inventory close-outs will always yield the best results.

9. Viral Marketing

The term viral marketing describes any strategy that encourages individuals to pass on a marketing message to others in the same way people pass viruses to each other. Friends are sending links to view YouTube videos and Dove had over 7,000,000 people view a message about natural beauty called "Evolution," SoCalled a Klezmer-Hip-Hop artist, has had over 1,500,000 views for his song/video.

10. Web Optimized Public Relations

We have been having tremendous success "optimizing" press releases so that they get picked up in Google and the other search engines. This is similar to search engine optimization, select three keyword phrases to target in the release, add the phrases to the headline and sub headline and throughout the body copy in the release. Add the press release to your website for 1-2 days before putting it on the wire. Use a traditional wire service or PR Web, which gets great results in Google for just $80, and link the wire release to your website.

The Beginner's Guide to Twitter – Ten Steps

Twitter is a 'microblogging' tool in which you can provide updates to others that choose to follow you. Originally, each update usually answered the question, 'What are you doing?' Now Twitter has evolved to include breaking news, helpful tips, business messages and words of wisdom, all limited to 140 characters.

Twitter has become incredibly popular and it is doubling in size each month! Originally a personal application, Twitter is an increasingly valuable tool for business and a great way to follow breaking news. For example, Twitter users always break news stories first such as the recent jet landing in the Hudson River. It is also a fun way to follow friends and celebrities. You can click here for a list of the top 50 celebrities on Twitter including Brittney Spears, Shaquille O'Neal and the first to have 1,000,000 Twitter followers, Ashton Kutcher.

Here's a beginner's guide to Twitter with ten steps to getting started and some advanced ways to use Twitter for business or personal branding.

Step #1 – Sign Up Now! (Get your name before it's gone!!!)

This is easy, go to Twitter.com and create your account. It is free! Reserve your name if it's available or select a 'brand name' that is consistent with your other social media identities. If it is still available reserve your company name at an alternate email address (each Twitter name must have a unique email address). Names are going fast; it is like the domain name rush of the mid 90's so make sure you protect your name and company name ASAP!

Step #2 Create a Basic Profile

Start with a simple description about yourself and good close headshot. Once you have a basic profile you may want to make it more creative or business-like by adding logos and backgrounds.

Definitely include a link to your website or Blog. When people find your profile they'll read your past 'tweets' and click the link to your website to decide whether they want to follow you.

Step #3 – LISTEN FIRST!

As you would in any new environment, come in to Social Media and 'listen' before you speak, or in the case of Twitter, read before you type. Get a feel for how people use 140 characters. What are the leaders in your niche regularly Twittering about? Recognize how rarely popular people on Twitter actually promote themselves. Similar to the best practices for networking, 'Give to Get!' When you give away great content, great ideas, great links, breaking news etc. you will get a large and loyal following.

To get started, have look at some of the popular people on Twitter and search for other folks who are influential in your field of interest. It is easy to find people who are connected, when you look at one person's Twitter screen you will be able to see everyone that they are following. So, if you look at http://www.Twitter.com/JayBerkowitz and hover your mouse over the images on the right, you'll see the folks I am following. CNNBRK is CNN Breaking News, if that would be of interest to you, click on the icon and you'll see a history of their most recent posts. If you'd like to follow CNNBRK simply click the 'follow' icon on their page and you'll see all of their 'Tweets' on your 'Home' twitter screen.

Please note - I recommend holding off on following too many people until you've built some good content on your Twitter page.

Step #4 – Write Some GREAT Tweets

When you follow people they get an email with a link to your Twitter page. They'll have a quick look and decide whether they are going to follow you. Set a strategy for what you are gong to communicate about. If you share daily dribble about what you had for breakfast and how long you had to wait in line at the grocery store most people who aren't very close friends won't follow you. If you share smart insights and links in your area of passion or specialty you will steadily build your following.

Some ideas for great tweets include commenting on big news in your area of specialty or expertise, linking to popular blogs or Tweets (short for a Twitter post) with added insight, sharing tips or valuable suggestions, Re Tweet valuable tweets by experts (see below for more on ReTweeting).

Don't spam! When you reply in DM (direct message) or post Tweets make them useful and never simply message another Twitter user just to get them to follow your links. Spam is ugly in any platform and will turn off your followers and maybe even get you booted from the platform altogether. Spam is never the most effective way to market. Make informative posts, pique your reader's interest and they will follow, and they will click your links because they are curious, not annoyed.

Step #5 – Follow the Leaders

A site called TwitterGrader.com lists the top Twitterers based on a simple algorithm, you can also identify the top people to follow in your area.

Here are some of the most well known Twitter internet marketing celebs www.Twitter.com/GuyKawasaki, www.Twitter.com/Scobleizer, www.Twitter.com/JasonCalacanis, www.Twitter.com/TechCrunch, www.Twitter.com/Mashable, www.Twitter.com/GaryVee, www.Twitter.com/LeoLaporte

Another great way to build your initial list of people to follow on Twitter is with a site called We Follow. This is a valuable site; you may search in your area of interest to find the top people by category.

Step #6 - RT (ReTweet) with an @ sign

The common practice in Twitter is to 'RT' or re-tweet messages and links that you want to share with your list, and when you do this you credit the original tweeter by mentioning their Twitter name with an @ sign. This practice often leads people to click the @name in your message to view the home Twitter page of the Twitter that you recognized. The better your tweets, the more re-tweets you get and hence the more traffic to your page. When you include the @name of a popular Twitterer they will likely track who is referencing them and come to check out who you are! Lastly, it is good form to thank people who RT and @ your Tweets.

Step #7 – Search.Twitter.com

The search function at Twitter is amazing, and fast. It is found at the top of your home page with the tab marking 'Find People'. That takes you to a page with four sections, one for finding people on Twitter by name, one for searching networks through your email for those who are already on Twitter, a section where you can invite those from your email lists to Twitter, and a final page with suggestions from the Twittersphere of popular members you may be interested in.

Twitter Search may propose the first significant risk to Google's market leadership as Twitter Search is instant. People search Twitter for what's being said on the Network, news, trends etc.

Step #8 Upgrade your profile

Your profile is your Twitter 'calling card'. It tells others about you in a nutshell and should be visually appealing as well as enticing. Try to inject your personality or an accurate feeling of your company in your profile description so that others are attracted to follow you. Add images and logos, company names and update with call-to-actions, offers etc.

Your Twitter image or avatar should depict you not just a logo. People are more drawn to personalities on a social network than they are a symbol or logo. They want to feel they know the person behind the logo or brand. The thing that makes social networking work so well is that potential consumers or clients feel they have a relationship with you and want to do business with the person. To add an image to your Twitter profile click on 'picture' from your settings area and you will be prompted to upload an image from your computer.

Your logo works great as a background and it is easy to include in the Twitter platform. Click on the 'settings' tab at the top of your Twitter toolbar. Then click on the 'design' tab at the top of the page and then click on 'change background image'. You will be prompted to scan your computer for an image that will upload to the back of your Twitter page.

Step #9 Upgrade your Twitter application

Can't be online to Twit? Don't worry you can still stay connected if you have a mobile phone. Twitter allows simple text updates to be sent through any cell phone. You can set it up from your 'settings' tab under the 'device' tab. Follow the prompts and then anytime you are away from your desk but want to send an update to 'what are you doing' you can.

That's not enough? Once you've Twittered for awhile you probably won't be satisfied with simply getting your Tweets on air from your phone but not be able to read what others are saying at the moment. You can do that too. The most common apps for that are for the iPhone but many other applications are available for most modern cell phones that will let you see your Twitter messages as they come in. There is also the 'Twitterberry' specifically for Blackberry users. At the very bottom of any Twitter page you will see a list of links.

You can add Twitter widgets to your blogs, your websites, and even your email so others can follow every Twit you Tweet. For your desktop you can incorporate an application like TweetDeck (http;//www.tweetdeck.com), one of the most popular Twitter applications that lets you get all of your incoming Tweets as well as make your own Tweets, and see direct messages, re-tweet, reply to direct messages right from your desktop without going to the Twitter page itself. TweetDeck has a large layout that shows you everything at a glance. Other smaller applications like Twirl are popular for those that only want to see incoming Tweets and Tweet back from their desktop without using up a lot of space.

Step #10 - Follow the Three E's of Social Media – Educate, Entertain and Engage!

If you are using Twitter for business or for building a personal brand and reputation, your followers will stay interested if you are a valuable place for information and links, I call this the first E of social media Educate.

The second E Engage encourages you to develop a two way dialogue with your users. Ask questions. Reply to their comments and happy and sad news. The Twitter celebrities have a Twitter timeline filled with @ replies and re-tweets as they engage in a two way dialogue with their followers.

Lastly, have fun. Entertain your followers with a funny YouTube video or a Blip.FM song selection once in a while. Going above and beyond and having some fun outside your niche keeps it light and lets your personality shine through.

You can post pictures to Twitter via a direct link to Twitpics, Visual Twitter, Twix[...] commonly used one is Twitpics. On Twitpics you can upload any picture from your computer and immediately send the link to it and a message to your T[...]

I regularly post amusing [...] but I recently drafted a list of the Top 50 Celebrities on Twitter. Don't be all business and try to use the Three E's of social media, beca[...]

Visit www.SocialMediaz.com/book to uncover the hottest new trends, and to disc[...] for business!

[Handwritten pink sticky note: "Can use iTunes Agent to listen to podcasts on Nook."]

94

Appendix

Recommended Watching, Listening and Reading for New Trends in Internet Advertising and Web Marketing

I think the most important development in "reading" is not reading at all but podcasting. I love podcasts, they allow me to time shift my learning and they are very entertaining. I listen to these podcasts while I'm commuting, working out and walking my dog; I turn previously brain-free time into stimulating learning. Podcasts have become my most important learning tool.

Podcasts

Ten Golden Rules Internet Marketing Podcast: http://podcast.tengoldenrules.com. The team at Ten Golden Rules shares the latest strategies and tactics for internet marketing and advertising.

The Daily Search Cast, http://dailysearchcast.com. Search engine marketing expert Danny Sullivan with a series of co-hosts. NOTE – this podcast is being updated infrequently.

Jaffe Juice, http://www.jaffejuice.com. Joseph Jaffe covers the latest in new media.

6 Pixels of Separation, http://www.twistimage.com/blog/podcast. Mitch Joel, with his audio community, is warm and engaging as he covers the latest new media and connectivity tools

That Affiliate Thing, www.WebmasterRadio.fm. The latest from the important field of affiliate marketing. Commentary, interviews, and various segments hosted by Lisa Picarille and Shawn Collins

For Immediate Release, http://www.forimmediaterelease.biz. Shel Holtz and Neville Hobson cover new marketing from the public relations perspective.

Marketing Over Coffee http://www.MarketingOverCoffee.com Christopher S. Penn and John Wall break down interactive marketing strategies over a Dunkin Donuts coffee.

DishyMix – Success Secrets with Famous Internet and Business Executives http://blogs.personallifemedia.com/dishymix . Susan Bratton interviews the internet elite.

Internet Business Mastery – www.internet-based-business-mastery.com Learn how to create a home based internet business

New Tools

Twitter

The latest flavor in social media is Twitter, www.Twitter.com . I describe it as instant messaging on steroids, many call it micro blogging. When you register to follow someone on Twitter, you see every "tweet" they post, a short message limited to 140 characters. I am following some of the leaders in internet media and business tweets such as CNN Breaking News, this is an incredible new way to get new news fast.

Video

How to videos and video blogs are emerging as powerful new communication tools. This incredible video, The Machine is Us/ing Us (Final Version), explaining Web 2.0 from Michael Wesch has made the assistant university professor one of the top speakers in the emerging industry
http://www.youtube.com/watch?v=NLlGopyXT_g&mode=related&search=

Audio and Video from the TED, conference http://www.TED.com, is simply the most amazing way to spend 18 minutes!

Video Podcasts from the Web 2.0 Summit feature major industry leaders at Tim O'Reilly's major industry event.
http://www.web2summit.com/pub/w/49/conversations.html

Scobilizer, http://scobleizer.com, Robert Scoble ex-Microsoft video blogger covers the latest tech tools and trends in interviews with the movers and shakers of Silicon Valley.

Social Media Networking

Social media networking sites allow you to create a network of contacts and are great for developing business networks and asking questions of your network.

LinkedIn, www.LinkedIn.com, is a fast growing networking site, the most remarkable feature how big your network expands at the second and third level of connections. I have 259 connections, these people have 67,100+ connections who have 2,715,400+ connections and I can ask my connections to introduce me to over 2 million of their associates!

Facebook, www.Facebook.com, founded by student Mark Zukerburg at Harvard, has grown rapidly since September 2006 when they opened to everyone. Facebook has exploded in popularity in 2007 by allowing people to add applications, small functions that let you interact with the site and its users.

Learn all about Facebook for Business on our podcast interview with Mari Smith
http://podcast.tengoldenrules.com/10goldenrules-podcast-episode36.html

Blogs / Websites

Blogs are the new e-newsletters. I subscribe to blog feeds and view headlines of my favorite blogs using Google reader. For the blogger, the subscription bypasses email and allows them to deliver their messages direct to the user with no spam interference.

Seth Godin's Blog, http://sethgodin.typepad.com. Seth Godin, author of several best selling marketing books is always on top of the trends that matter.

http://www.searchengineland.com. Danny Sullivan and the team at Search Engine Land cover the breaking news in the search marketing industry

Matt Cutt's Blog, http://www.mattcutts.com/blog. Google Engineer Matt Cutts is one of the most respected experts in the search engine space.

10 Golden Rules Internet Marketing Strategy Blog, http://tengoldenrulesblog.blogspot.com. Covers the latest internet marketing strategies to get more traffic to websites and convert that traffic to leads and sales.

Influential Marketing Blog, http://rohitbhargava.typepad.com. Rohit Bhargava is intellectual and educational.

Micro Persuasion, http://www.micropersuasion.com. Steve Rubel always has the big stories in internet and PR and he explains why they matter.

http://www.clickZ.com. Click Z has a range of internet marketing topics including search email and emerging trends.

Books

Any book written by Seth Godin. My recent favorite, "Meatball Sundae," brings back many of his past themes such as permission marketing and makes them current.

"Don't Make Me Think", Steve Krug, an extremely well written book about website usability, the name says it all. A recent new edition features three new chapters.

"The Long Tail: Why the Future of Business is Selling Less of More," Chris Anderson the editor in chief of Wired magazine created the best catch phrase of internet selling, he explains the how Amazon and other online retailers have opened the door to 'long tail' books, movies and audio recordings that wouldn't have had a market in the pre-wired world.

"Wikinomics, How Mass Collaboration Changes Everything," Don Tapscott and Anthony D. Williams explains how open architecture is changing business, particularly the internet.

"The Search - How Google and Its Rivals Rewrote the Rules of Business and Transformed our Culture," John Battelle explains the history of search marketing and the key insight that allowed Google, a late starter to become the dominant player in the industry.

"Life After the 30-Second Spot: Energize Your Brand With a Bold Mix of Alternatives to Traditional Advertising," the colorful Joseph Jaffe explains how traditional approaches to marketing aren't relevant in a new media world.

"Winning Results with Google AdWords," Andrew Goodman explains how to succeed in the hypercompetitive world of Google Pay-Per-Click advertising.

"Search Engine Visibility," Shari Thurow wrote a classic book on the basics of designing a website for free search engine pick up.

"Analytics an Hour a Day," Google Analytics Evangelist Avinash Kaushik shows you how to make website Analytics a powerful tool.

"How to Do Everything with Podcasting," Shel Holtz and Neville Hobson give you the nuts and bolts of this important, expanding craft.

"Presentation Zen," If you do any PowerPoint presenting, Garr Reynolds will take you to the top of the game.

"Six Pixels of Separation," Mitch Joel distills internet marketing into simple sound bites. This book targets a CEO not internet marketing professionals.

"Trust Agents," Chris Brogan and Julien Smith with a fascinating take on the new media economy.

"The New Rules of Marketing and PR," David Meerman Scott with a great analysis of the evolution of marketing and public relations.

ProBlogger: Secrets for Blogging Your Way to a Six-Figure Income." Darren Rowse and Chris Garrett are professional bloggers and they share their secrets.

"Word of Mouth Marketing: How Smart Companies Get People Talking," Andy Sernovitz leans towards traditional marketing, some great approaches for the online world as well.

"Twitter Power," Joel Comm with a great explanation of the new world of Twitter.